Margaret Barker is an independent scholar, a Methodist local preacher and a former President of the Society for Old Testament Study. She has developed 'Temple Theology' as a new approach to biblical studies, and was given a DD for her work on the temple and the origins of Christian liturgy. For many years, she has been a member of the Ecumenical Patriarch's Symposium on Religion, Science and the Environment, and has made Temple Theology the basis for her work on the environment.

Her recent books include: *Temple Themes in Christian Worship* (2008), *Christmas: The Original Story* (2008), *The Hidden Tradition of the Kingdom of God* (2007), *Temple Theology* (2004), *An Extraordinary Gathering of Angels* (2004), *The Great High Priest* (2003) and *The Revelation of Jesus Christ* (2000).

TEMPLE MYSTICISM

An introduction

MARGARET BARKER

First published in Great Britain in 2011

Society for Promoting Christian Knowledge
36 Causton Street
London SW1P 4ST
www.spckpublishing.co.uk

British Library Cataloguing-in-Publication Data
A catalogue record for this book is available from the British Library

ISBN 978–0–281–06483–0
eBook ISBN 978–0–281–06702–2

Typeset by Graphicraft Ltd, Hong Kong
First printed in Great Britain by Ashford Colour Press
Subsequently digitally printed in Great Britain

Produced on paper from sustainable forests

For Bruce Clark

Christ, by whom the eyes of the blind recover sight, will shed on you a brighter light than the sun . . .

O truly sacred mysteries, O pure light. My way is lit with torches and I see the heavens and God. I become holy as I am initiated. The LORD is the revealer of the mysteries, He marks the initiated with his seal and illuminates him. He commends the believer to the Father, to be kept safe for ever . . .

If you wish, you also can be initiated, and you will dance with the chorus of angels around the unbegotten and imperishable only true God. The Word of God will join with us in our hymn.

Clement of Alexandria, *Exhortation to the Greeks* 12

Contents

Preface

Temple mysticism underlies much of the Bible, but it has not been formally acknowledged. I have wanted for some time to collect key texts and ideas, and thus try to recover the ancient system from the scattered fragments that remain, from the echoes and from the shadows.

It soon became clear that much of the system was implicit, and had to be recovered from the underlying assumptions of familiar texts. Doubtless many other texts were lost or suppressed, but there was also oral tradition. Some teachings were not written down even by the literate, because they were secret; others were not written down because they were the collective memory of people who were not literate. The people in Egypt who challenged Jeremiah's theology (Jer. 44.15–23) were refugees from first temple Jerusalem, and they saw things very differently from Jeremiah or his later editors. They did not write down their 'theology', and we have only hints as to what it was. It is not our place, with the wisdom of hindsight and the viewpoint of later orthodoxy, to say who was 'right' and who was 'wrong'.

The Enoch tradition, even though we have it in written form, condemned writing as an invention of the fallen angels (*1 Enoch* 69.9–10). The ancient high priests, among whom 'Enoch' had his roots, were the only ones with access to the holy of holies and its meaning (Num. 17.7). The laity did not even enter the temple, and so they did not see the furnishings, they did not watch the rituals and they did not hear the sacred words and teachings. These three represent the elements of an ancient mystery religion: the things shown, *deiknumena*, the things done, *drōmena*, and the things spoken, *legomena*. The accounts of the mystery religions, however, are from sources written later than the Hebrew scriptures, and Clement of Alexandria was no innovator when he described Christianity, the heir to the original temple, as a mystery religion.

When the cult of the first temple was destroyed at the end of the seventh century BCE, the priesthood was scattered, and their teachings went with them. Elements of the older ways spread far and wide. They survived in systems that would be labelled 'gnostic' and in texts that would be labelled 'non-canonical'. By apportioning labels like this, the evidence was filtered, and an artificial construct was presented as the religion of ancient Jerusalem. The parts of early Christianity that differed from it were deemed the influence of Greek philosophy, especially Platonism. This, as we shall see, was a serious distortion.

There was an early Eucharistic prayer: 'As this broken bread, once dispersed over the hills, was brought together and became one loaf, so may thy church be brought together from the ends of the earth into thy kingdom' (*Didache* 9). I hope this little book will help gather together the scattered fragments of temple mysticism that gave the original vision of the kingdom and flowered to become what we know as Christianity.

My thanks, as always, go to my family who understand computers, to the staff of the Cambridge University Library, and to my friends. I should like to dedicate this book to one of those friends, who may not agree with every word of it.

Margaret Barker

Introduction

Temple mysticism is the key to understanding Christian origins, but there is no single text or passage in the Bible that answers the question: What is temple mysticism? We have to reconstruct it from the gaps in our understanding of Christian origins, rather like working out what part of the picture would have been on the missing piece of the jigsaw puzzle. The difference is that we do not have the picture on the lid of the jigsaw box, and so cannot be certain what the missing piece – or rather pieces – looked like. One missing piece would be a simple matter. Indeed, some of the pieces already put into the puzzle may be in the wrong places, or even in the wrong puzzle.

Temple mysticism is a hypothesis. We outline what seems to have been the case and then see how much of the evidence fits the proposed picture, how many texts make more sense and cohere better if they are read in this way. There can be no proof, but temple mysticism does give new answers to important questions: who did Jesus think he was and what did he think he was doing; how did the Christians understand their new faith; and how did they express this in their worship?

As a brief introduction to the subject and the method, I shall examine some well-known texts in the light of temple mysticism. The texts are from Isaiah, the prophet whom Jesus quoted more than any other scriptures, and from John, who was close to Jesus and would have understood him as well as anyone. Tracing just this one line of texts gives remarkable results; and there is a whole Bible waiting to be reread.

Isaiah

In the year that King Uzziah died, Isaiah saw the Lord sitting upon a throne, high and lifted up, and his robe filled the temple. John explained to the readers of his Gospel that Isaiah had seen Jesus in glory (John 12.41). Isaiah saw six-winged *seraphim* standing above the throne and he heard them calling out to each other: 'Holy, holy, holy is the LORD of Hosts; the whole earth is full of his glory.' The sound made the whole building shake, and the prophet was overcome

1

with the sense of his own sin and unworthiness: 'For my eyes have seen the King, the LORD of Hosts' (Isa. 6.1–5).

Isaiah's vision is the earliest dateable evidence for temple mysticism – the death of Uzziah has been put anywhere between 759 and 739 BCE – and this brief account includes enough detail to establish that temple mysticism, as known in much later sources, was a feature of the first temple in the eighth century BCE. John identified the enthroned figure of Isaiah's vision as Jesus in glory, showing that Jesus' closest disciples understood him in the context of temple mysticism, and, indeed, identified him as the figure at the very centre of the mystical vision.

Temple mysticism, however, has been eclipsed in the study of the Hebrew scriptures by another movement which came to dominate both the ancient transmission and collection of the scriptures and much of the modern scholarship devoted to their study. Deuteronomy denied that the LORD could be seen, and in the Deuteronomists' account, when the commandments were given to Moses 'you heard the sound of words, but saw no form' (Deut. 4.12). The other version of Moses receiving the commandments says that he and others saw the God of Israel (Exod. 24.10), and we can only assume that the writer of Deuteronomy was contradicting this. Seeing the LORD – temple mysticism – was both controversial and, apparently, suppressed.

In the investigation proposed in this book, which of necessity is text-based, the suppression of ancient source material is a huge problem. Some evidence can still be detected, but the process of recovering temple mysticism is far from easy.

Let us begin with Isaiah's vision. The prophet saw the LORD enthroned and heard him speak. This must have been in the holy of holies, whose other name was the *d*ᵉ*bir* (1 Kings 6.5, 16 etc.; 2 Chron. 4.20; Ps. 28.2). As often happened with temple terms, the first Greek translation (the Septuagint, hereafter LXX) simply transliterated the word as *dabeir*, but later versions translated it as 'oracle', the place where the LORD spoke.[1] The LORD appeared to the high priest in the incense cloud above the mercy seat (Lev. 16.2), and the LORD spoke to Moses 'from above the mercy seat, from between the two cherubim

---

[1] Thus Aquila, Symmachus, *chrēmatistērion*, and the Vulgate *oraculum*. The current fashion is to derive it from another word and translate 'inner room'.

that are upon the ark of the testimony' (Exod. 25.22; also Num. 7.89). In the desert tabernacle, which is the setting for these verses, the mercy seat with its two *cherubim* was behind the veil, that is, in the holy of holies (Exod. 40.20–21), and it had the same function as the throne which Isaiah saw in the temple. His contemporary Hezekiah prayed 'O LORD of Hosts, God of Israel, who art enthroned above the cherubim . . .' (Isa. 37.16). The ark under the mercy seat was the footstool of the throne. David had planned to build a temple 'for the ark of the covenant of the LORD, and for the footstool of our God' (1 Chron. 28.2); and the psalmist sang of bringing the ark to Jerusalem, 'Let us go to his dwelling place; let us worship at his footstool' (Ps. 132.7).

Whether or not Isaiah was literally in the holy of holies is not relevant; he saw the LORD enthroned there. Since it was only the high priest who could enter the holy of holies, and then only once a year on the day of atonement (Lev. 16.2–5), it is significant that Isaiah associated his vision with purging his sin. A *seraph* took a burning coal from the incense altar and purified the prophet's 'unclean lips'. Isaiah had the experience of a high priest, and so it is likely that he *was* a high priest and received his vision on the day of atonement.

Isaiah saw that the edges of the LORD's robe, his 'train', filled the *hēkal*, the outer part of the temple which corresponds to the nave of a traditional church. In temple cosmology, this part of the temple represented the visible creation, and so Isaiah saw the LORD's train extending from the throne in the holy of holies and out into the material world. The Lxx of Isaiah has 'the house was filled with his glory', showing that the train of the LORD was a way of describing his glory, and the Aramaic translation[2] also says that the *hēkal* was filled with the brightness of the glory.

Elsewhere this word 'train' was used for the skirts of the harlot city (Lam. 1.9; Jer. 13.26; Nahum 1.9), but also for the edges of the high priest's robe. The Priestly writer in Exodus described pomegranates and golden bells that decorated the 'train' of the high priest's robe (Exod. 28.33–34; 39.24–26), and since Isaiah's vision was set in the temple, it is likely that the 'train' of the LORD's robe was like that of the high priest. The earliest prescription for the high priest's garments was that they were 'for glory and for beauty' (Exod. 28.2), and for

---

[2] The Targum of Isaiah, which is a translation augmented by additional detail, showing how the Hebrew text of Isaiah was understood in the time of Jesus.

centuries the memory persisted that the robes of the high priest had been cut from the LORD's robe of heavenly glory.[3]

Isaiah also saw *seraphim*, whose name means 'burning ones'. Elsewhere in the Hebrew scriptures, the *seraphim* are snakes: 'a flying serpent' (Isa. 14.29; 30.6; also Deut. 8.15). The story of Moses and the fiery snakes uses various words for 'snake' including *seraph*, and it seems that the bronze snake on a pole, which Moses set up to protect the people, represented a *seraph* (Num. 21.6–9). Jesus compared his own 'lifting up' on the cross to the lifting up of this *seraph*, but the original significance of his saying is lost. The *seraph*/bronze snake was still used in worship in the time of Isaiah, until it was destroyed by Hezekiah, the last of the kings under whom Isaiah prophesied (2 Kings 18.4; Isa. 1.1). Each of the *seraphim* that Isaiah saw had six wings, and so Isaiah described the holy of holies as filled with fiery beings. The Targum described them as 'servants'. The *seraphim* in the holy of holies are not mentioned elsewhere in the Bible, and so perhaps they appear under another name.

The *seraphim* were calling out, and this is another feature of the mystics' experience. The visions were never silent. As they saw the glory, so they heard the sound of the holy of holies. Isaiah described the song as

> Holy, holy, holy is the LORD of Hosts;
> The whole earth is full of his glory.

The message of the heavenly beings was that the glory of the LORD filled the earth, and it was one of the fundamentals of temple mysticism that only those who had glimpsed the glory in heaven could see the glory on earth. The song of the *seraphim* (hereafter 'the Sanctus') was heard by John when he too stood in his vision before the throne (Rev. 4.8), and it became a part of the Christian liturgy. This is a vivid reminder that Christian liturgy has its roots in temple mysticism, the worshippers joining with the heavenly beings in the holy of holies.

> Therefore with Angels and Archangels, and with all the company of heaven, we laud and magnify thy glorious Name; evermore praising thee, and saying:

---

[3] We shall return to this; see below, p. 137.

Holy, holy, holy, Lord God of Hosts, heaven and earth are full of thy glory: Glory be to thee, O Lord most High.[4]

Isaiah saw the temple filled with smoke, perhaps in reality the smoke of incense that the high priest took with him into the holy of holies, but the prophet described it with a word that implies the LORD's anger, '*ashan*, as in 'O LORD of Hosts, how long will you be angry, *smoke*, against the prayers of your people?' (Ps. 80.4, my translation). His reaction was fear and a sense of his own great sin, a sin committed with his lips. The detail is lost, but a sin of the lips does imply false teaching, something that he shared with his people: 'I am a man of unclean lips and I dwell in the midst of a people of unclean lips.' The *seraph* purified his mouth with a burning coal from the altar, and then the Lord asked: 'Whom shall I send, and who will go for us?' Isaiah replied: 'Here am I! Send me.' Presumably the purified prophet would deliver the true teaching.

The temple mystics were messengers from heaven to earth; their vision was not just a private ecstasy, but always a call to be the bearer of revelation. This explains the enigmatic words to Aaron and his sons, the high priestly family: 'And you and your sons with you shall attend to your priesthood for all that concerns the altar and that is within the veil; and you shall serve' (Num. 18.7). They were the servants of the LORD, with access to whatever lay beyond the veil in the holy of holies, and this included the teachings from and about the holy of holies. Malachi reminded the negligent priests of his own time that they had been called to be 'messenger[s] of the LORD of Hosts' (Mal. 2.7). Messengers from heaven are more commonly called angels – it is the same word in Hebrew – and so the temple mystics were angels on earth.

Hecataeus, a Greek writing about 300 BCE, described the Jewish high priest in just this way: for the Jews, he said, their high priest was an angel of God's commandments, and when he spoke to them, they immediately fell to the ground and worshipped him as he explained the commandments to them.[5] Jesus ben Sira, a Jerusalem Jew writing about 200 BCE, said something very similar of the high priest Simon:

---

[4] From the Communion Service in the Book of Common Prayer of the Anglican Church.
[5] Hecataeus, quoted in Diodorus of Sicily, XL.3.5–6.

5

> How glorious he was . . . as he came out of the
>   house of the veil! . . .[6]
> When he put on his robe of glory
> And clothed himself with superb perfection
> And went up to the holy altar
> He made the court of the sanctuary glorious . . .
>   (Ben Sira 50.5, 11)

It has sometimes been said that Matthew was wrong to describe Jews worshipping Jesus, for example, after he calmed the storm on Galilee (Matt. 14.33). No Jew would have 'worshipped' another human being, and so Matthew must have been reading later beliefs back into his telling of the story. But if people recognized Jesus as an angel on earth – and they did – then Matthew's account could have been accurate.

The message Isaiah had to deliver is the only clue as to what the false teaching had been. The people would hear and not understand, see and not perceive, and the reason for this must have been the rejection of Wisdom, since Wisdom gave understanding and perception. Next there is an oracle in what is called chiastic form, using wordplay that is characteristic of temple discourse.

> A Make the heart of this people *fat*,
>   B And their ears *heavy*,
>   C And *shut* their eyes;
>   C Lest they see with their eyes,
>   B And hear with their ears,
> A And understand with their heart,
>   And turn and be healed.

The centre of this oracle is loss of sight, in this case, spiritual blindness. There is another account of these events in a brief, stylized history preserved in *1 Enoch*: 'all who live in it [i.e. the temple] shall be blinded, and the hearts of all of them shall godlessly forsake Wisdom, and in it a man shall ascend . . .'[7] The priests in the temple lost their 'sight' and forsook Wisdom, and Isaiah ascended, presumably to stand before the heavenly throne.

The wordplay in this oracle reveals both sides of the prophet's message, but is completely lost in translation. The heart means the

---

[6] The house of the veil was the holy of holies, so this happened in the day of atonement.
[7] *1 Enoch* 93.8.

mind, and 'fat', *shemen*, is a word whose various forms can mean either fat in the sense of prosperous and arrogant, or the anointing oil, as prescribed for use in the tabernacle (Exod. 30.24) or for anointing the king, 'the oil of gladness' (Ps. 45.7). The wordplay implies the contrast of an anointed mind or an arrogant mind. 'Heavy', *kabōd*, is the same word as 'glory', and the wordplay implies the contrast of ears that hear the glory or are deaf to it. 'Shut' is literally 'smeared over', *sha'a'*, a word that sounds very like *sha'ah*, meaning 'look to' the LORD (e.g. Isa. 17.7; 31.1), and so the wordplay contrasts eyes that look to the LORD with eyes that are smeared over and cannot see. Now eyes that were smeared with holy oil were symbolically opened, and so in the ideal state, the mind and the eyes would be anointed and the ears would hear the glory. All this had been lost due to false teaching, and the punishment for those who followed the false teaching was to live with what they had chosen. They would be deprived of understanding, and so of repentance and healing. Most of this has also been lost in translation.

How long would this last, asked Isaiah, and here we see another characteristic of the temple mysticism texts: they are often damaged and no longer readable. Sometimes it is possible to reconstruct them by comparing other ancient translations such as the Greek, but often there is very little that can be restored. This 'damage' to temple texts is so frequent that it cannot have been coincidence. Here, Isaiah hears the heavenly voice warning that the loss/rejection of Wisdom will continue until the land is desolate, until 'the forsaken places are many in the midst of the land', a line whose Hebrew can also mean: 'And great is the Forsaken One in the midst of the land.' The history in *1 Enoch* says that Wisdom had been forsaken, and so it is likely that Isaiah received an oracle about the restoration of Wisdom, when perception would return. The final verse of Isaiah's call vision – now incomprehensible – has 'a tenth' remaining, the stump of an oak tree and the holy seed. This was formerly a description of Wisdom under her ancient names and symbols, the one in whom was the holy seed. 'A tenth' is a word very similar to Ashratah, one of her ancient names, the tree was her symbol, and she was the 'mother' of the Messiah, the holy seed.

Recovering temple mysticism is not easy, but this brief reading of Isaiah's call vision shows how much of the style and the later elements can be detected even in the eighth century BCE: the vision of the

LORD, the glory, the throne, the heavenly beings, the song, the human standing before the throne to receive teaching, and Wisdom lost and restored, and the wordplay. These also appear in the book of Revelation, especially if the Greek text is returned to the Hebrew or Aramaic of the original: the song of the heavenly beings round the throne; the servants standing in the holy of holies before the LORD enthroned; the tree of life and the river of life restored, both symbols of Wisdom; and the bitter wordplay contrasting what was with what should be, the present reality and the vision.

John

John quoted this oracle about lost perception to explain why some people did not accept the teaching of Jesus, and he linked it to another passage in Isaiah, his poem about the Servant that was re-used by a later disciple and is now found in the middle section of the book. Often described as the Song of the Suffering Servant (Isa. 52.13—53.12), the poem describes an unnamed figure whose identity has been much debated. The poem applies certain expectations to a historical figure, and it seems that Isaiah had been in two minds about him. The Servant was at first despised and rejected, presumably by Isaiah, who then realized that he was fulfilling the LORD's plan in a way that the prophet had not expected: 'yet it was the will of the LORD to bruise him . . .' (Isa. 53.10). The most likely figure to have prompted Isaiah's reflection on suffering was Hezekiah, who, when the Assyrians were threatening Jerusalem, was himself at the point of death and rejected by the prophet. Isaiah then changed his mind and realized that the stricken king would live and see Jerusalem delivered from the Assyrians (Isa. 38.1–22).[8]

John's linking of these two passages – the call vision and the Song of the Suffering Servant – was not random. Both were applied to Jesus: Isaiah saw the pre-incarnate Jesus when he saw the LORD enthroned, and the Song of the Suffering Servant was used to interpret the death and resurrection of Jesus, even by Jesus himself (Luke 24.25–27). Together with Psalm 110, another temple mysticism text, the Song is the most quoted passage in the New Testament. It also has much

---

[8] See my article 'Hezekiah's Boil', *Journal for the Study of the Old Testament* 95 (2001), pp. 31–42.

in common with Isaiah's call vision. This shows that the early Christians identified the Servant and the one enthroned amid the *seraphim*.

The Song of the Suffering Servant implies a set of expectations by which Isaiah interpreted the events of his time. The Song begins: 'My servant shall be given understanding, he shall be high and lifted up and shall be very high' (Isa. 52.13, my translation). The Greek is 'My servant shall have understanding . . .'[9] 'He was high and lifted up' are the same words as in the throne vision, where it was Isaiah who received the gift of understanding. The present Hebrew text[10] says the servant was 'marred beyond human semblance', and describes his suffering and rejection when people thought that his plight was punishment for sin. Then the prophet realized that the servant was the sin bearer and that his sufferings were to protect his people.

Isaiah must have known of a servant figure who – perhaps in ritual – had to suffer and pour out his life as a sin offering. *Key words in this text have been damaged or removed.* The Targum knew that the figure was 'my servant the Anointed One', and the Christians saw in this passage an important prophecy of the suffering of Jesus, the Anointed One. The MT does not mention anointing. The great Isaiah scroll found at Qumran, however, has an extra letter in the word 'marred' – 'his appearance was marred beyond human semblance' – so that it could be read as 'anointed'. The servant would then be 'anointed beyond human appearance, his form beyond that of a human being', in other words, a man transfigured by anointing. This would explain why the Targum and the early Christians thought this poem was about the Anointed One, and why the Targum went on to explain that the servant did not look like a common man but had a holy brightness or splendour.[11]

Nor does the MT mention 'the light' that the Servant saw after his suffering. The Lxx reads: 'It was the will of the Lord . . . to show him light and to form him with understanding' (Lxx Isa. 53.11), and the Qumran texts of Isaiah[12] also say that he saw the light. The words in the Qumran Hebrew that are not in the MT identify the Song of

---

[9] The Hebrew *śakal* usually means 'have prudence or understanding', and sometimes 'prosper'.
[10] The Masoretic text, hereafter MT.
[11] Targum to Isaiah 53.2.
[12] 1QIsa^a, 1QIsa^b and 4QIsa^d Lxx.

the Suffering Servant as a temple mysticism text: the Anointed One who was high and lifted up, saw the light and was given knowledge. Furthermore, it was the Qumran version of this Song that Jesus quoted to the disciples on the road to Emmaus: 'Was it not necessary that the Anointed One should suffer these things and enter into his glory?' (Luke 24.26, my translation). There is no text in the MT that prophesies the Anointed One suffering and entering the glory. *Jesus must have known the version of Isaiah found at Qumran*, and the Christians who gave Luke the material for his Gospel must have known that Jesus used the Song of the Suffering Servant as a prophecy of himself.

The Song inspired an early Christian hymn. Writing to the Philippians, Paul included a passage about Jesus as the Servant which is widely thought to be a quotation:

> Christ Jesus . . . emptied himself, taking the form of a servant . . . and became obedient to death, even death on a cross. *Therefore* God has exalted him and bestowed on him the name that is above every name, that at the name of Jesus every knee should bow, in heaven and on earth and under the earth, and every tongue confess that Jesus Christ is LORD, to the glory of God the Father.
>
> (Phil. 2.5–11, my translation)

'Emptied himself' is the Servant pouring out his soul (Isa. 53.12), and the 'therefore' shows that the hymn, like the original Servant Song, was written according to a well-known pattern. Humility and death do not naturally result in exaltation and the highest honour. 'Therefore' must refer to the underlying pattern. There was an expectation that the Servant who poured out his soul would be exalted – 'high and lifted up' – but the Christian hymn gives additional information not explicit in the Servant Song.

The exalted Servant was given the name above every name, in other words, he was given the name Yahweh, and so all creation in heaven and earth bowed before him and acknowledged that Jesus the Anointed One was the LORD, that is, Yahweh.[13] This appears in the book of Revelation as the vision of the Lamb[14] who was enthroned and then worshipped by all creation (Rev. 5.6–14). John knew that the One

---

[13] 'The name of Jesus' means 'the name that Jesus was given'.

[14] Lamb and Servant are equivalent terms, as we shall see, p. 135.

whom Isaiah had seen enthroned, high and lifted up, 'the LORD of Hosts', was the man he had known as Jesus. This transformation, the human being raised up and becoming divine, was the very heart of temple mysticism.

John described Jesus praying after the last supper, just before he went out across the Kidron to the garden where he was arrested. This was, in effect, the climax of Jesus' teaching, recorded by John who was probably the disciple 'whom Jesus loved' and present at the supper (John 13.23). They may not be his precise words, but John has preserved clear evidence that Jesus saw himself as a high priest in the tradition of the temple mystics.

Jesus prayed, 'Father, glorify thou me in thy own presence with the glory which I had with thee before the world was made' (John 17.5). The setting is temple cosmology: the glory is the state represented by the holy of holies, the invisible creation that is outside both time and matter. Jesus knew that he had been in that state before the visible creation was formed in time, and he knew he was returning to that state. He knew he was the 'one LORD, through whom are all things' (1 Cor. 8.6, my translation), that 'He was in the beginning with God; all things were made through him, and without him was not anything made that was made' (John 1.2–3). 'The beginning' was another way of describing the holy of holies and what it represented.

We shall return to this prayer later,[15] but suffice it at the moment to note some of the characteristics of temple mysticism. 'That they may be one, even as we are one' (John 17.11). Unity was at the heart of temple teaching: the holy of holies represented this unity, which was the origin of all creation. The account of creation in Genesis begins with the separation of the pre-created light from the darkness on Day One, the original unity (Gen. 1.3–5).[16] The process of creation was separation – the firmament separated the waters, the heavenly lights separated day from night (Gen. 1.7, 14); and distinction – 'each according to its kind' (Gen. 1.12, 21, 24). The bonds of the great covenant held the creation together, and they were sealed by the Name. The Many were a Unity through the Name.

---

[15] See below, p. 70.

[16] Not 'the *first* day'. The ancient texts are unanimous that it was Day One, the day of unity.

Thus Jesus prayed: 'Keep them in thy Name, which thou hast given me, that they may be one, even as we are one' (John 17.11). Through his disciples, Jesus would extend this unity:

> I do not pray for these only, but also for those who believe in me through their word, that they may all be one; even as thou, Father, art in me, and I in thee, that they also may be in us, so that the world may believe that thou hast sent me. (John 17.20–21)

Unity was both the sign and the proof of divine origin. Jesus had brought the glory into the material creation, and some people had recognized this – 'We have beheld his glory' (John 1.14) – just as Isaiah had learned that the whole creation was full of the glory. The disciples also became vehicles of the glory, and this was another sign and proof of divine origin:

> The glory which thou hast given me I have given to them, that they may be one even as we are one, I in them and thou in me, that they may become perfectly one, so that the world may know that thou hast sent me . . . (John 17.22–23)

Jesus prayed that his disciples would join him and see him in his glory:

> Father, I desire that they also, whom thou hast given me, may be with me where I am, to behold my glory which thou hast given me in thy love for me before the foundation of the world. (John 17.24)

Jesus was praying that his disciples would stand where Isaiah had stood, to see him in the glory of the pre-created light, in the holy of holies that was the beginning of all things and so the state before the creation of the material world.

John saw this in his final vision of the throne (Rev. 22.1–5). He had seen the new Jerusalem as a huge golden cube (Rev. 21.15–18), in other words, as a huge holy of holies which had no temple because it was itself the temple. In the midst of the holy of holies was the throne of God-and-the-Lamb, John's way of describing the Lamb who had become divine. Flowing from the throne was the river of life that watered the roots of the tree of life. These, as we shall see, were symbols of Wisdom, and so John saw Wisdom restored to the holy of holies. The servants of God-and-the-Lamb worshipped him and saw his face. His name was on their foreheads. Now the Name on the forehead meant only one thing: they were all high priests, and so they had all entered the holy of holies to stand before the throne in the presence of the LORD: 'Let us then with confidence draw near to the throne of grace . . .' (Heb. 4.16).

John's vision is the earliest 'picture' of Christian worship. The servants, the new collective high priesthood, stand before the throne in the pre-created light. 'They shall reign for ever and ever' means the royal priesthood restored. Peter described them as 'a chosen race, a royal priesthood, a holy nation, God's own people . . . called . . . out of darkness into his marvellous light' (1 Pet. 2.9).

Just as Isaiah had become a messenger from the LORD when he stood before the throne, so too had John. The letters to the seven churches are the earliest Christian texts,[17] sent from Jerusalem to the Christians of Asia Minor. John had received them from the risen LORD, who appeared to him as a radiant figure in the temple, the LORD making his presence shine for him (Num. 6.24–26). All the letters show that temple mysticism was the common framework for early Christian discourse: eating from the tree of life, conquering the second death, eating the hidden manna and receiving a new name, being appointed as the Morning Star,[18] wearing white garments, opening eyes with holy oil, and sharing the heavenly throne (Rev. 2.7, 11, 17, 28; 3.5, 12, 18, 21).

Temple mysticism is the key to understanding Christian origins: what Jesus knew himself to be, how the early Christians understood their new faith (or rather, their recovery of the old faith) and how they expressed this in their worship.

---

[17] See my book *The Revelation of Jesus Christ*, Edinburgh: T&T Clark, 2000, pp. 69–70.

[18] 'I will give him the Morning Star' is an over-literal rendering of the Semitic idiom 'I will appoint him as the Morning Star'.

1

The sources

The first source for temple mysticism is the temple itself and what it represented. There are several descriptions of the temple in the Bible (1 Kings 6—8; 1 Chron. 28.11–19; 2 Chron. 3—6) and the detailed accounts of building and erecting the desert tabernacle also include features from the temple (Exod. 25—40). Outside the Bible there are the writings of Josephus, who described the desert tabernacle[1] and the temple he knew in the first century CE;[2] and those of Philo, his older contemporary, who often mentions the temple and its symbolism. There are also writings such as *1 Enoch*, which the first Christians regarded as Scripture but are no longer in the Bible of most churches. The Enoch tradition is especially valuable for our quest, because much of what it records is temple tradition. Or so it seems. Many 'temple' texts do not proclaim themselves as such, and so the process of recovering the temple and its mystical tradition can mean reconstructing a possible context for apparently isolated texts.

One of these reconstructions is as certain as anything can be: the tabernacle and the later temple were built to represent the creation. Ancient sources differ as to the detail, but the six stages of erecting the tabernacle correspond to the six days of creation. The books of Moses begin with his vision of the creation, and so Genesis 1 describes Moses' six-day vision on Sinai (Exod. 24.16). Then the LORD spoke to him from the cloud and told him to build a tabernacle according to what he had seen on the mountain (Exod. 25.9). The account of erecting the tabernacle (Exod. 40.16–33) corresponds to the six days of creation in Genesis 1.[3] The holy of holies screened by the veil represented the beginning of creation, and the outer part of the tabernacle represented the visible creation of the third to sixth days.

---

[1] Josephus, *Antiquities* 3.102–207.
[2] Josephus, *War* 5.184–237.
[3] Each stage is marked in Exodus 40 by 'As the LORD commanded Moses.'

Only the high priests were allowed to enter the holy of holies, and they alone knew the meaning of the holy of holies at the heart of creation. The matters 'within the veil' were entrusted to them alone (Num. 18.7), and so, apparently, was the meaning of the sacred furnishings and vessels. Origen (died 253 CE), a Christian biblical scholar writing in the early third century, said that even the Levites were not allowed to see the tabernacle objects. The high priests had to wrap them before the Levites were allowed to transport them (Num. 4.5–15).[4] Jewish tradition said that the furnishings of the original temple had been lost or hidden away in the time of King Josiah (late seventh century BCE), and would be restored in the time of the Messiah: the seven-branched lamp, the ark, the *cherubim*, the Spirit and the fire, according to one version;[5] the anointing oil, the manna, the ark and Aaron's rod according to another.[6] In other words, the teaching of the original temple had been lost and would be restored in the time of the Messiah.

The Qumran texts mention the hidden teaching or lost teaching; the community considered themselves the faithful remnant, to whom God had revealed 'the hidden things in which all Israel had gone astray. He unfolded before them His holy Sabbaths, and his glorious feasts, the testimonies of his righteousness and the ways of his truth . . .' God rebuilt their community, the priests who remained faithful when others went astray. They were 'destined to live for ever, and all the glory of Adam shall be theirs'.[7] Another text spoke of teachers who had been hidden and kept secret',[8] and Josephus said that the Essenes took an oath to reveal none of their secrets, to preserve their books and the names of the angels.[9] Temple mysticism, then, was the preserve of the original high priesthood, and the Christians emphasized that Jesus was their great high priest who had passed through the heavens, that is, the veil (Heb. 4.14). Texts about the holy of holies were also hidden away: the words of some familiar biblical texts, as we have seen, had another form that referred to the

---

[4] Origen, Homily 5 *On Numbers*.

[5] *Numbers Rabbah* XV.10.

[6] Babylonian Talmud *Horayoth* 12a.

[7] *Damascus Document* CD III.

[8] 11Q Melchizedek, as translated in F. Garcia-Martinez, ed., *Discoveries in the Judean Desert* XXIII, Oxford: Oxford University Press, 1998, p. 229.

[9] Josephus, *War* 2.142.

mystical teachings of the temple; and a story written down in the early Christian period, about 100 CE, shows that many sacred texts were deliberately concealed and kept only for the wise.

The story is that Ezra, a Jew who came to Jerusalem from Persia in the fifth century BCE, heard a divine voice speaking to him from a bush, telling him that he was, in effect, the new Moses.

> I led [Moses] up on Mount Sinai, where I kept him with me many days; and I told him many wondrous things, and showed him the secrets of the times and declared to him the end of the times. Then I commanded him, saying, 'These words you shall publish openly, and these you shall keep secret.'   (2 Esd. 14.4–6)

This distinction between secret things and what could be taught to everyone was not new. As early as Deuteronomy, Moses had said: 'The secret things belong to the LORD our God; but the things that are revealed belong to us and our children for ever, that we may do all the words of this law' (Deut. 29.29). The Deuteronomists did not deny the existence of 'secret things'; but they questioned their relevance to the everyday business of life and keeping the Law.

Ezra complained that the Law had been burned when Jerusalem was destroyed by the Babylonians, and that nobody knew of the great works the LORD had done. He was then told to take five scribes and, inspired by the Most High, to dictate the lost books to them.

> So during the forty days ninety-four books were written. And when the forty days were ended, the Most High spoke to me, saying, 'Make public the twenty-four books that you wrote first and let the worthy and the unworthy read them; but keep the seventy that were written last, in order to give them to the wise among your people. For in them is the spring of understanding, the fountain of wisdom, and the river of knowledge.' And I did so.   (2 Esd. 14.44–48)

Ezra had to restore everything, but only about a quarter of the holy books would be for public reading. Most of the inspired texts, according to this story, were only for the wise. Since the 24 were the Hebrew scriptures, *this story shows that the most important teachings – understanding, wisdom and knowledge – were not in the Hebrew scriptures.*

The *Mishnah*, collected about 200 CE, preserves the traditions and customs of the late second temple period. Among them are listed the passages of canonical scripture forbidden for public reading or for public explanation. Some were scandalous passages, for example the story of Reuben taking his father's concubine (Gen. 35.22), the story of Tamar seducing her father-in-law (Gen. 38.13–19), and the story of David and Bathsheba (2 Sam. 11.2–17). Others were forbidden for another reason; they were temple texts about the holy of holies: Ezekiel's vision of the chariot throne (Ezek. 1.4–28), the story of the beginning of creation (Gen. 1.1–3), and even the high priestly blessing which prayed for the LORD's presence to shine forth (Num. 6.24–26).[10] The Aramaic translation of Numbers sometimes left these verses in the original Hebrew, because people were not to know about them.

The story of 70 secret books is consistent with this custom of not reading or expounding certain passages of Scripture. What is interesting for our enquiry is that the Christians clearly did know and use these forbidden temple passages: Ezekiel's chariot throne vision has echoes in Revelation, and the LORD's presence shining forth was John's great proclamation: 'We have beheld his glory' (John 1.14). It was also the Christians who preserved the Jewish story of Ezra knowing more books than were in the Hebrew canon and hiding them away, and it was the Christians who preserved the non-canonical Hebrew texts. Who, then, was Ezra?

Ezra

The original Ezra was sent by the king of Persia in the fifth century BCE to re-establish the Jewish community in Jerusalem. King Artaxerxes sent 'Ezra the priest, the scribe of the law of the God of heaven' (Ezra 7.12) to enforce 'correct' religious beliefs and observances. Exactly when he came is not known, as the chronology of the books Ezra–Nehemiah is not clear, but the story is that he read out the Law to the assembled people of the city, and the Levites helped the people to understand. Thus Ezra the priest restored the scriptures to his people, and his Levites gave the official interpretation (Neh. 8.1–8). This was a new role for the Levites; according to the Chronicler, David had appointed them originally as temple musicians, to praise and thank the LORD, and to invoke his presence (1 Chron. 16.4). *Ezra was*

---

[10] Mishnah *Megillah* 4.10; Mishnah *Ḥagigah* 2.1.

associated with the restored written text and with its meaning. 'Ezra' the high priest and scribe became a symbolic figure; just as Moses gave the Law, so Ezra restored the scriptures.

Ezra himself is a mystery. He was not mentioned by Ben Sira in his list of famous men, where the great figures of the early second temple period are Zerubbabel, Joshua and Nehemiah (Ben Sira 49.11–13). Nor is his genealogy beyond suspicion. Ezra was presented as a high priest, but the family line was altered. According to one high priestly genealogy, the line was Azariah, Seraiah, Jehozadak who was taken into exile, then Joshua, the high priest who returned from exile (1 Chron. 6.14; Hag. 2.2). According to Ezra's genealogy, the line was Azariah, Seraiah, Ezra (Ezra 7.1); Jehozadak and Joshua have gone. 'Ezra' and his scriptures replaced the old high priestly line just as his Levites had a new role as interpreters of the text rather than as musicians calling on the divine presence.

The more detailed account of Ezra restoring the scriptures is found in 2 Esdras, which is the older Jewish *Apocalypse of Salathiel*, expanded and then preserved by Christian scribes.[11] The scriptures were restored 30 years after the fall of Jerusalem, and we are invited to believe that this was the first destruction of the city in 586 BCE. In fact, the story was written after the second destruction in 70 CE, but 'history repeating itself' was a well-known literary style. 'Ezra' restoring the scriptures was really describing how they were collected and preserved around 100 CE, and this story was part of the original Jewish *Apocalypse of Salathiel*. It is not known if there was a formal process at this time to collect and preserve the scripture, led by the rabbis at Jamnia ('The Council of Jamnia'),[12] but the emperor Vespasian did allow this centre of Jewish learning to survive the destruction,[13] and the scholars there must have been involved.

There were three developments. First, the canon of Hebrew scriptures was defined. There is no precise list of what books were considered holy in the time of Jesus; Josephus said there were 22 books: 5 books of Moses, 13 of history and prophecy, and 4 of hymns and guidance for life, but none is named.[14] The current way of counting the Hebrew

---

[11] In the Vulgate it is named 4 Esdras. The Christian additions are cc.1–2 and 15–16.
[12] Also called Yabneh or Jabneh.
[13] Babylonian Talmud *Gittin* 56b.
[14] Josephus, *Against Apion* 1.8.

scriptures and the Ezra story give 24 books.[15] Did Josephus divide the books differently, or did he know a different list? At Qumran there is evidence for 21 copies of Isaiah and 30 of Deuteronomy, but none for 1 Chronicles and Nehemiah,[16] and none for Esther. There is, however, evidence for 20 copies of *1 Enoch* and 15 of *Jubilees*, and it is likely that both *1 Enoch* and *Jubilees* were Scripture in the Qumran library, but again, there is no list. Fifty years after the destruction of the temple, R. Akiba taught that anyone reading the excluded books would have no place in the world to come,[17] and so there must have been a recognized canon of Hebrew scripture by his time. Furthermore, not only had the canon of Scripture been defined by the early second century CE, but the other books, presumably the books for the wise, were prohibited.

Second, the form of the Hebrew text was fixed. It is sometimes said that the text of the Hebrew scriptures 'stabilized' after about 100 CE, but this is not a natural process like decay or regrowth. *It means that someone stabilized it.* The scripture texts found at Qumran are sometimes different from those that became the MT, and it is reasonable to ask what criteria determined the eventual form of the text that was chosen by the stabilizers and became the 'standard' Masoretic text. There is good reason to believe that the MT was a text chosen from several available alternatives and that some of the older readings were removed or changed in response to the claims of Christianity.

Some of the evidence for this is that new Greek translations of the Hebrew text were made in the second century CE.[18] The Christians had adopted the old Greek translation, the Lxx, which had originally been accepted by the Alexandrian Jewish community as a miraculously accurate translation of the Hebrew text. Anyone who changed it would be cursed.[19] By the second century CE, however, the Lxx translation was condemned: 'The day of its translation was as grievous for Israel as the day when the golden calf was made . . .'[20] The Lxx was no longer thought to be accurate, and so the new Greek translations were necessary. *This can only mean that the Hebrew text*

---

[15] The 12 minor prophets are one book.
[16] Although they may have been part of a larger scroll.
[17] Mishnah *Sanhedrin* 10.1.
[18] The translations of Theodotion, Aquila and Symmachus.
[19] *Letter of Aristeas* 311; Philo, *Moses* II.40.
[20] Mishnah *Soferim* 1.7.

*used for the Lxx had been superseded, such that the older Greek no
longer represented the current Hebrew.* 'Christian' terms were avoided;
Aquila, for example, would not use the word *christos*, anointed, in
any Old Testament text, but made a new word *eleimmenos*, oiled.

Furthermore, it was ruled that any scrolls written and used by
minim, i.e. Christians, had to be destroyed, and should not be rescued
from a fire.[21] 'The revelations, *gilyonim*, and the books of the *minim*
do not defile the hands', i.e. are not sacred.[22] 'Revelations' then were
characteristic of the Christians, and the Jews mocked them with bitter
wordplay: *evangelion*, the Greek word for gospel, was pronounced as
two similar sounding Hebrew words *avon gilyon*, meaning 'iniquitous
revelation', or *aven gilyon*, 'worthless revelation'.[23]

The process of altering scripture was not new. Sometimes described
as 'rewritten scripture', the practice shows how the holy texts were
used as vehicles for new interpretation and teaching. A comparison
of well-known texts shows that the story of David and Bathsheba
is found in 2 Samuel 11 but not in the corresponding part of
1 Chronicles. The story showed David in a bad light. Descriptions
of the holy of holies in 1 and 2 Chronicles do not appear in 1 Kings,
as we shall see. The return of the exiles from Babylon – Ezra being a
leading figure[24] – was described by *1 Enoch* as the return of blinded
sheep whose temple service was polluted, a generation of apostates.[25]
The Third-Isaiah, who prophesied at this time, described the leaders
of the temple as 'his watchmen', but blind and without knowledge,
shepherds without understanding (Isa. 56.10, 11). The final chapters
of *1 Enoch* warn of sinners altering the texts: 'Woe to those who
tamper with the words of truth and distort the eternal covenant and
yet consider themselves without sin.' 'Sinners will tamper with and
distort the words of truth and pervert many . . .'[26] As was the custom
in these texts, nobody was named, but the events were recorded.

Certain scribes were authorized to 'restore' the text, changing passages that they deemed blasphemous or inappropriate. Traditionally,

---

[21] Babylonian Talmud *Gittin* 45b, Tosefta *Shabbat* 13.5; Tosefta *Yadaim* 2.13.
[22] Tosefta *Yadaim* 2.13.
[23] Babylonian Talmud *Shabbat* 116a. The line is censored from some editions.
[24] The accounts of the period are disorderd, but see Ezra 8—10 and Nehemiah 8.
[25] *1 Enoch* 89.73–4; 93.9.
[26] *1 Enoch* 99.2; 104.10, translation by D. Olson, *Enoch*, North Richland Hills: Bibal Press,
2004.

there are 18 of these *tiqqune sopherim*,[27] restorations of the scribes, and the scribes claimed the authority of Moses for the changes: 'Words read but not written, words written but not read, all these are *halachah* from Moses at Sinai.' All the later conventions for reading the text and 'fixing' its meaning, they said, went back to the work of Ezra described in Nehemiah 8.8: ' "They read from the book, from the law of God" refers to scripture, "clearly" refers to the Targum, "and they gave the sense" refers to the division into sentences, "so that the people understood the reading" refers to the accents or, some say, to the *masoroth*.'[28] These latter were originally the bonds or fetters (as in Ezek. 20.37) by which the meaning of the text was fixed, but later the word was said to come from *masar* meaning to hand down, in other words, the traditional reading.

The work of these scribes was sophisticated and governed by strict rules. Existing letters could be rearranged, and one letter (even two) could be replaced by another. One of the list of 'eighteen' corrections is found three times: a dispersing army was told to return 'each man to his tents' (2 Sam. 20.1, my translation; 1 Kings 12.16; 2 Chron. 10.16). The original had been 'each man to his God', but this implied polytheism in Israel and so it was removed by transposing the two letters *l* and *h*: *l'lhyw*, 'to his God', became *l'hlyw*, 'to his tents'. Sometimes the change was to remove an offensive name: Saul's son was Eshba'al, man of Baal (1 Chron. 8.33), but changing the two final letters made it Ishbosheth, man of shame (2 Sam. 2.8). Sometimes the theological motive is clear: 'Let us make man in our image' became 'I will make man . . .' by changing one letter. There were 13 of this type of alteration, made when the Lxx was translated, said Jerome, so that King Ptolemy of Egypt would not think there had been mystical prophecies of the Messiah and that the Jews worshipped a second God.[29] So too with the 'sons of God' in the Song of Moses, clearly the ancient angels of the nations. Here two letters were changed and the sons of God became in the MT the (in context) incomprehensible 'sons of Israel'. Both the Qumran text and the Lxx have the original 'sons of God' (Deut. 32.8). The scribes changed *h* and *m* for *ś* and *r*, making *'lhym*, God, into *yśr'l*, Israel.

---

[27] Also spelled *tikkune soferim*.
[28] Both are quotations from Babylonian Talmud *Nedarim* 37b.
[29] Jerome, Preface to *Hebrew Questions on Genesis*; also in Jerusalem Talmud *Megillah* 1.9.

These scribes were associated with Ezra and a body known as the 'men of the Great Synagogue'.[30] The tradition was that a group of 120 elders, including some prophets, came back from exile with Ezra and re-established the correct rules for observing the Law. This group was, in effect, the bridge between the prophets and the later teachers of the Law. 'Moses received the Law from Sinai and committed it to Joshua, and Joshua to the elders, and the elders to the prophets, and the prophets committed it to the men of the Great Synagogue.'[31] Simon the Just[32] was the last of the original body, but the tradition of teaching and interpreting the Law continued for centuries. The heirs of the 'Great Synagogue' were responsible for deciding which books (and which versions) should be included in the canon, and their changes could well have prompted Jesus' remark that with his teaching, not even the smallest letter would change in the Law (Matt. 5.18). An *agraphon*, a saying not found in the Gospels but attributed to Jesus, was: 'Become experienced bankers', meaning that his followers had to recognize forgeries, to distinguish true from false Scripture.[33]

The heirs of the Great Synagogue were responsible for establishing how the oral law, also given by Moses on Sinai, was to be studied and observed, and Jesus, according to Mark, criticized the 'tradition of the elders' for losing sight of the commandments of God through their concern for 'the tradition of men', 'making void the word of God through your tradition' (Mark 7.5–8, 13).

They were also responsible for establishing the forms of synagogue worship, especially the 'Eighteen Benedictions'. Nobody knows when these Benedictions were composed, but R. Gamaliel II, the great teacher of the Jamnia period, said they should be prayed every day.[34] It was in his time that a nineteenth was added, the so-called 'benediction for heretics' which was, of course, a curse on them.[35] Now positioned twelfth in the list, one version from this period prays

---

[30] Or 'the great assembly'.

[31] Mishnah *Aboth* 1.1.

[32] Probably the Simon mentioned in Ben Sira 50.1–21, about 200 BCE.

[33] This is found in the *Clementine Homilies* 2.51; 31.50; 18.20; also in Clement of Alexandria, *Miscellanies* 1.28.

[34] Mishnah *Berakoth* 4.3.

[35] Babylonian Talmud *Berakoth* 28b says the curse on the *minim* was instituted at Jamnia.

that Christians, *noṣerim*, and heretics, *minim*, should perish and be blotted out of the book of Life.

This, then, was the heritage of 'Ezra', who is said to have known but kept hidden certain holy books, and whose genealogy was composed such that he took the place of Joshua (that is Jesus) as the high priest who restored temple worship in Jerusalem.

The great high priest

During this period when the Jews were stabilizing their scriptures, collecting and writing their oral law, and cursing the 'heretics' in the synagogues, the Christians were also telling their story.

First, they claimed to be the heirs of high priestly teaching, and that Jesus had taught with authority and not like the scribes (Mark. 1.22). Many priests joined the Church in Jerusalem (Acts 6.7), and Jesus was proclaimed as a great high priest (Heb. 4.14). James and John (but not Peter) were remembered as high priests who had worn the golden seal engraved with the divine name.[36] This implies that the Christians had a parallel to the temple hierarchy, and a tradition of secret teaching associated with the holy of holies. Ignatius, bishop of Antioch around 100 CE, taught: 'To Jesus alone as our high priest were the secret things of God committed.'[37] Clement of Alexandria, writing a century later, distinguished true Christian teaching from false using the same holy of holies imagery: 'they do not enter in as we enter in, through the tradition of the LORD, by drawing aside the curtain . . .'[38]

There was another *agraphon*, quoted by Peter in a book attributed to Clement of Rome: 'We remember that our LORD and teacher, commanding us, said: "Keep the mysteries/secrets for me and the sons of my house." Wherefore also he explained to his disciples privately the mysteries of the kingdom of heaven.'[39] There are hints of this in the Gospels, when Jesus explained to his inner circle why he taught in parables: 'To you has been given the secret of the kingdom of God, but for those outside everything is in parables' (Mark 4.11). The kingdom, as we shall see, was the holy of holies and

---

[36] Eusebius, *History of the Church* 3.31; Epiphanius, *Panarion* 1.29.
[37] Ignatius, *To the Philadelphians* 9.
[38] Clement, *Miscellanies* 7.17.
[39] *Clementine Homilies* 19.20, also quoted in Clement of Alexandria, *Miscellanies* 5.10.

what it represented. Jesus then quoted the oracle to Isaiah about the punishment for rejecting Wisdom: they would see and not perceive, hear and not understand. They would not see the kingdom.

The Christians also knew of sealed books and scrolls that had to be eaten, that is, scrolls of secret teaching. John saw the One on the throne holding a book sealed with seven seals.[40] The description is not clear, but it seems that the Lamb took his place on the throne at the same time as he took the book, and then all creation in heaven and earth worshipped the Lamb who was holding the sealed book (Rev. 5.1–14). After the seven seals had been opened, the mighty angel brought the opened book[41] and gave it to John, who was told to eat it and then speak as a prophet (Rev. 10.1–11). This sequence – the Lamb receiving the book and opening it, and then the mighty angel bringing the book to John – is summarized in the first verse of Revelation. 'The revelation of Jesus Christ, which God gave to him to show to his servants what must soon take place' means that the visions were given to Jesus who had to reveal them to the 'servants of God'. This is the vision of the Lamb receiving the book and opening the seals. 'And he [Jesus] made it known by sending his angel to his servant John' means that Jesus entrusted/explained the meaning of his visions to John. This is the vision of the mighty angel bringing the opened book to John.

Recognizing that Jesus himself received visions in the manner of temple mystics, and that these form the core of Revelation, is important for recovering temple mysticism and for establishing its key role in the early Christianity. John implies in his Gospel that Jesus had received visions before he began his public ministry: 'He who comes from heaven is above all. He bears witness to what he has seen and heard, yet no one receives his testimony' (John 3.31–32). He also implies that there will be more revelation in the future:

> I have yet many things to say to you, but you cannot bear them now. When the Spirit of truth comes, he will guide you into all the truth; for he will not speak on his own authority, but whatever he hears he will speak, and he will declare to you the things that are to come.
>
> (John 16.12–13)

---

[40] The Greek *biblion* can be either book or scroll.
[41] The Greek word is *biblaridion*, a little book.

He defined the early Christian community as the other offspring of the woman clothed with the sun (in addition to the Messiah), those who kept the commandments of God and who had the testimonies of Jesus, already defined as 'the things that he saw' (Rev. 12.17, translating literally, and Rev. 1.2).

There are glimpses elsewhere of Jesus the temple mystic: he saw the heavens open at his baptism (Mark 1.10), and the heavenly voice named him as the divine Son. Origen knew that at his baptism, Jesus saw the chariot throne that Ezekiel had seen by the River Chebar (Ezek. 1.4–28).[42] Jesus then spent 40 days in the wilderness 'with the wild beasts and the angels served him' (Mark 1.13, my translation). He was alone and so must have reported these experiences to others, and presumably not in Greek. This is important because in Hebrew, the 'wild beasts' would have been the same word as the 'living creatures' of the chariot throne, *hayyot* (Ezek. 1.5; Rev. 4.6), and the serving angels would have been the worshipping hosts in the throne vision since 'serve', *'ābad*, also means 'worship' in Hebrew (Rev. 5.11). Jesus' mystical experience in the desert is described more fully in the opening scene of Revelation: he took the book, was enthroned among the living creatures and then served/worshipped by the angels (Rev. 5.1–14). Thus it was that John could say of him at the very start of his ministry: 'He bears witness to what he has seen and heard . . .' and could claim that the Christians kept these testimonies (Rev. 12.17).

When Ezekiel saw the fiery chariot throne and its attendants by the River Chebar, this must have been how he envisaged the holy of holies. His experience is important for understanding what is written between the lines in the New Testament, and for glimpsing what the early Christians might have understood when they read the same words as we read. An early illustrated gospel, for example, shows the Ascension as Jesus being taken up in the chariot that Ezekiel saw.[43] Some said there had been a fire in the Jordan when Jesus was baptized.[44] This was a sign of the chariot vision, since fire had appeared

---

[42] Origen, Homily 1 *On Ezekiel.*

[43] The Rabbula Gospels, sixth-century Syrian. The Ascension can be seen on p. 111 of my book *An Extraordinary Gathering of Angels*, London: MQ Publications, 2004.

[44] Two Old Latin versions of Matthew 3.15, Codex Vercellensis and Codex Sangermanensis; Justin, writing in Rome in the mid-second century CE, *Trypho* 88: and Ephrem, writing in Syria in the late fourth century CE, *Commentary on the Diatessaron.*

when a disciple of the R. Johanan ben Zakkai (a contemporary of Jesus) was expounding the mysteries of the chariot throne.[45]

Ezekiel saw the One seated on the chariot throne, a fiery human figure wreathed in a rainbow. The figure offered him an open scroll to eat and then told him to speak to people who would not listen (Ezek. 2.1—3.11). Origen commented:

> Our prophets did know of greater things than any in the Scriptures, which they did not commit to writing. Ezekiel, for example, received a roll written within and without . . . but at the command of the Logos he swallowed the book in order that its contents might not be written and so made known to unworthy persons. John is also recorded as having seen and done a similar thing.[46]

Note that Origen thought that the fiery human figure on the throne was the Logos, the Second Person, another feature of temple mysticism, and this is clearly the same figure as the mighty angel whom John saw offering him the little book to eat (Rev. 10.1). After eating the scroll, Ezekiel was lifted up by the Spirit and carried away to his people (Ezek. 3.12–15). Origen knew of the *Gospel according to the Hebrews*[47] which says that Jesus too was carried away by the Holy Spirit, described as 'his mother', and taken to Mount Tabor.[48] We cannot know how much of this underlies the brief Gospel descriptions of Jesus' baptism and time in the wilderness, but temple mysticism is very much the context of the ministry of Jesus the great high priest.

Whose Bible?

There are many versions of the Old Testament, and the Hebrew-based English translations are different in several important ways from anything that Jesus or the early Church would have known. Any attempt to reconstruct or to understand Christian origins that is based on the Old Testament found in English Bibles is less likely to succeed than one that is more broadly based. We now look at how Christian writers told the story of forming the Old Testament canon.

---

[45] Jerusalem Talmud *Ḥagigah* 77; Babylonian Talmud *Ḥagigah* 14b.
[46] Origen, *Against Celsus* 6.6.
[47] Now lost apart from quotations in ancient writers.
[48] Quoted in Origen, *On John* 2.12; and Homily 15 *On Jeremiah*.

Justin, a convert to Christianity, wrote his *Dialogue with Trypho* in the mid-second century CE. He was setting out the points of disagreement between Jews and Christians at that time, and Trypho the Jew may or may not have been a historical figure. Justin came from Samaria; he was born about 100 CE and raised about 40 miles away from Jamnia, the centre of Jewish learning. His comments to Trypho about the changes being made to the Hebrew scriptures are therefore of considerable interest. First, he knew of the Greek translations being made to replace the older Lxx, by that time deemed by the Jews to be the golden calf that led Israel astray.

> I certainly do not trust your teachers when they refuse to admit that the translation of the scriptures made by the seventy elders at the court of King Ptolemy is a correct one and attempt to make their own translation. You should also know that they have removed entire passages from the version composed by those elders.[49]

He also knew that they had rejected the word 'virgin', *parthenos*, for the unnamed mother in Isaiah 7.14, and said it should be 'young woman', *neanis*.[50] 'Virgin' had been acceptable to the Jewish community in Alexandria when the older translation was made – perhaps they still remembered who the woman was – and so it must have been Christian use of the text that necessitated the new translation. Justin also claimed that passages had been removed from Jeremiah and the Psalms. Before the discovery of the Qumran biblical texts, it was said with some confidence that the 'differences' between the Lxx and the current Hebrew text were Christian additions, inserted to add weight to the prophecies of Christ. This can no longer be considered as a possibility.

The Qumran texts have shown beyond reasonable doubt that what Justin claimed did happen. Texts to verify or otherwise the actual examples he gave to Trypho have not been found, but many others do confirm that Hebrew texts of special interest to Christians were changed or disappeared. One of the proof texts at the beginning of Hebrews is in the Lxx and in a Qumran fragment,[51] but 'Let all God's angels worship him' (Lxx Deut. 32.43; Heb. 1.6) is not in the MT.

---

[49] Justin, *Dialogue with Trypho* 71.
[50] Justin, *Trypho* 71.
[51] 4QDeut^q.

This key verse shows that Jesus was identified as Yahweh, the first born. Yahweh, the LORD, is not usually identified as the firstborn son, but that was the original belief. Yahweh was the son of God Most High – as Gabriel announced to Mary (Luke 1.32) – and so the Hebrew scriptures witness to Father and Son. The Christian proclamation 'Jesus is LORD' meant Jesus is Yahweh. The human manifestation of the LORD, the son of God Most High, was at the heart of temple mysticism, but was one of the crucial pieces of evidence that did not become part of the MT. Nor did the verse about God Most High dividing the nations among 'the sons of God', of whom Yahweh received Jacob (Deut. 32.8). The sons of God became in the MT the incomprehensible 'sons of Israel'. There are many examples, as we shall see, in the course of reconstructing temple mysticism.

Origen wanted to establish the correct text of the scriptures. He collected all the known versions in his huge work set out in six colums, the 'Hexapla'. It is likely that this work was compiled as a basis for discussion with Jews. He was all too aware of differences between the Jewish and Christian scriptures in his time and took care 'so that in our debates with the Jews we do not use passages that are not in their texts and so that we do not use those passages which are in their texts but not ours'.[52] Note that he agreed to debate the issue *on the basis of the Jewish canon and text forms, but he did not intend that these should become the Christian scriptures.* 'Should we suppress the texts used by the churches and order the community to reject the sacred books which they use and flatter the Jews and persuade them to give us pure texts in their place, without any forged additions?'[53] Origen assumed that the Hebrew text he was given was the original; he was not aware of the variety of older Hebrew texts, and consequently he 'corrected' the LXX that the Christians were using in the light of both the post-Christian Hebrew and the three later Greek translations made from it. The result was a disaster for any knowledge of the original Christian scriptures.

And then there was Jerome. When he was asked by Pope Damasus to make a new Latin translation, around 400 CE, he chose the post-Christian Hebrew text as the basis for his work. Augustine warned

---

[52] Origen, *Letter to Julius Africanus* 5(9).
[53] Origen, *Letter to Julius Africanus* 4(8).

him that this was a mistake, since it implied that the Greek text was less valuable than the Hebrew.[54] Jerome went ahead, using both the current Hebrew text and the Hebrew canon. His reason? So that the Jews would not be able to say that the Church had false scriptures.[55] Again, a Christian writer had accepted the Jewish canon and text in the interest of 'discussion' with the Jews, and as a result, all Bibles based on Jerome's work, and those from the Reformation based directly on the post-Christian Hebrew text, are not the Old Testament as Jesus and the first Christians would have known it. What has been lost is temple mysticism, which is the key to understanding Christian origins.

Some early Christian writers quote 'Scripture' that cannot now be found in the Old Testament. The *Letter of Barnabas*, for example, a Christian text from the second or third generation,[56] quotes frequently from unknown scriptures: 'A heart that glorifies its maker is a sweet savour to the LORD'; 'I am now making the last things even as I made the first'; 'If my sons keep the Sabbath I will show mercy upon them' and many more.[57] Of considerable interest is a quotation about the day of atonement sacrifice that would link it directly to the original understanding of the Eucharist. 'And what does it say in the prophet. "Let them eat of the goat which is offered for their sins at the fast, and [note this carefully] let all the priests but nobody else, eat of its inward parts, unwashed and with vinegar."' Jesus drank vinegar just before he died, said Barnabas, to prepare himself as the atonement sacrifice that the priests consumed.[58] This would explain why the Eucharist has the imagery of consuming blood, an otherwise un-Jewish practice. Blood was consumed with the unwashed sacrifice on the day of atonement. Thus the Eucharist is not drawn just from Passover, but, as set out in Hebrews, from the day of atonement also (Heb. 9.11–14). But which 'prophet' was Barnabas quoting, and why has this crucial 'temple' text not survived elsewhere?[59]

---

[54] Letter preserved in Jerome, *Letters* 104.

[55] Jerome, Preface to Isaiah: '*ne Iudaei de falsitate scriptarum ecclesiis diutius insultarent*'.

[56] It is included at the end of the Sinai Codex, which contains the oldest complete copy of the New Testament.

[57] *Letter of Barnabas* 2, 6, 15.

[58] *Letter of Barnabas* 7.

[59] There is a hint of the practice in Mishnah *Menaḥoth* 11.2, that in some circumstances the Jews of Babylon used to eat the atonement goat raw.

The Christians were also expelled from the synagogues, just as the 'blessing on the *minim*' required. Justin, who was born in Samaria and had lived in both Ephesus and Rome, said this many times in his debate with Trypho. 'You curse in your synagogues all those who are called from him Christians, and other nations effectively carry out the curse by putting to death those who simply confess themselves to be Christians.' 'You curse [Jesus] without ceasing, as well as those who side with him, while all of us pray for you and for all men, as our LORD and Christ has taught us to do' (cf. Matt. 5.44).[60] This was the situation in the mid-second century but it was not new. Paul had taught that nobody who cursed Jesus could claim to be inspired, whereas anyone who proclaimed 'Jesus is the LORD' was speaking with the Holy Spirit (1 Cor. 12.3, my translation). John linked expulsion from the synagogue with recognition that Jesus was the LORD (John 12.41–42), and Jesus warned his followers that the Jews would consider it a pious duty to kill them (John 16.2). Thus he could say that Jerusalem the harlot city was drunk with the blood of the saints and martyrs (i.e. witnesses) of Jesus (Rev. 17.6), and that the heavens rejoiced when Jerusalem was burned, when the LORD avenged the blood of his servants (Rev. 19.1–3, alluding to the mutilated text Deut. 32.43).

This is the history that makes any quest for early source material so difficult.

The hidden Wisdom

Ezra's 70 books, therefore, are very important. As with the public canon of 24 books, no list of them survives, and we have to sift among the other material that seems to belong to this period and to this context. Some of the books may be represented among the Dead Sea Scrolls, such as the otherwise unknown *Book of Hagu*, which was compulsory study for members of the Qumran community.[61] There are also books of Wisdom teaching which have been pieced together and published under various titles,[62] the many fragments of

---

[60] Justin, *Trypho* 96, 133, with similar sayings in 16, 47, 93, 95, 108, 123, 137.
[61] *Damascus Document* CD X.6; XIII.2; XIV.8; *Messianic Rule* 1QSa I.6.
[62] *4Q Instruction* and *Sapiental Work A* are two examples. The main pieces of text are 4Q416, 417 and 418, but there are many other Qumran fragmnents identified as 'wisdom'.

Enoch texts, the Temple Scroll, the various hymns and prayers and much more.

The first problem is labels and dating. Scholars labelled the canonical Hebrew texts as 'prophecy', 'wisdom', 'history' and so on, on the basis of the limited sample of material that became canonical. They dated them on the unacknowledged premise that canonical texts were as old as they claimed to be, but that all others were only as old as the oldest known physical evidence for them. Thus Isaiah in the eighth century BCE could not possibly have known *1 Enoch*, for which there is no manuscript evidence until the mid-second temple period. The earliest manuscript evidence for Isaiah is rather later, but this was not mentioned. The first misgivings arose with the apocalyptic texts, when it became clear that the canonical apocalypse, Daniel, was in no way typical. What were all the hitherto unknown texts found at Qumran? Sectarian, it was assumed, because the canon was thought to determine 'orthodoxy' long before the canon existed. Other questions then arose: what criteria determined that one apocalypse but not another was accepted into that canon, one Wisdom text but not another, and so on. What, then, was the criterion for 'Ezra' keeping 'wisdom' texts away from the general public? 'In them is the spring of *understanding*, the fountain of *wisdom* and the river of *knowledge*' (2 Esd. 14.47).

The Wisdom texts in the Hebrew canon are Job, Proverbs and Ecclesiastes, together with a few psalms and passages in the prophets. In the Deutero-canonical texts ('the Apocrypha') there are the Wisdom of Jesus ben Sira (Ecclesiasticus), the Wisdom of Solomon, and parts of Tobit. It is possible that these texts are 'late' – second temple – and compiled by scribes as collections of traditional teaching; or they could be the work of scribes in the royal court and therefore from the first temple period. Material of similar style and content was produced by scribes in Egypt and Mesopotamia, and so scholars have toyed with ideas such as that of gentleman scholars of the ancient Jerusalem foreign office. What is clear is that the Wisdom texts in the Hebrew canon are only a remnant of the original wisdom; they have no concern with history or covenant, have a largely secular application, no real theology, and show no possible reason for Deuteronomy offering the Law as a replacement for Wisdom (Deut. 4.6).

It is likely that such Wisdom material as survived into the canon had been modified in the light of the later emphasis on the Law – 'Ezra' again. This is clear in the reworking of the great hymn in

Ben Sira 24, where the praise of Wisdom has been clumsily changed into praise of the Law of Moses (Ben Sira 24.23). The absence of theology in the canonical Wisdom texts was because no compromise was possible with the original Wisdom theology. There is no way that the platitudes of the Wisdom texts in the MT would have been reserved only for the wise because they were 'the spring of *understanding*, the fountain of *wisdom*, and the river of *knowledge*' (2 Esd. 14.47), but the speech of the archangel Raphael to Tobit and Tobias reveals the original context of these apparently isolated pieces of advice. At the end of the story, Raphael recites a sequence of Wisdom teachings: 'It is good to praise God . . . Do not be slow to give him thanks . . . Do good, and evil will not overtake you . . . A little with righteousness is better than much with wrongdoing . . .' (Tobit 12.6–8). He then reveals who he is: Raphael, who had been invisibly present when Tobit did each of his good deeds and who took his prayers (implying that his good deeds were the prayers) up into the glory of the Holy One. Wisdom was the teaching of the angels who then watched as the teachings became reality and thus a part of the glory on earth. In Revelation, John explained that the glorious garments in which the Bride appeared were the good deeds of the saints, another way of saying the same thing (Rev. 19.8).

The image of Wisdom as water – understanding, wisdom and knowledge – is also found in Ben Sira's poem about Wisdom, although now applied to the Law. Unfortunately, 2 Esdras is a Latin text and this part of Ben Sira is only known in Greek, so precise comparisons are not possible. Ben Sira's Wisdom compares herself to a river bringing *wisdom, understanding and knowledge* (Ben Sira 24.25–27),[63] and the context of the poem implies that this flows from the temple where Wisdom has her dwelling. Compare now Enoch's vision of the holy of holies, described as 'the vision of Wisdom.'[64] After seeing the heavenly counterpart of the day of atonement, he described the ever-flowing fountain of righteousness and the many fountains of wisdom that were flowing near the throne, so that the thirsty could drink from them.[65] This is the context for 'Let him who is thirsty

---

[63] Using P. W. Skehan's translation in *The Wisdom of Jesus ben Sira*, Anchor Bible, New York: Doubleday, 1987.
[64] *1 Enoch* 37.1.
[65] *1 Enoch* 48.1.

come, let him who desires take the water of life without price' (Rev. 22.17); for 'Blessed are those who hunger and thirst for righteousness' (Matt. 5.6); and for Jesus' invitation: 'If any one thirst, let him come to me and drink.' He then quoted from Scripture we no longer have: 'Out of his heart [i.e. his mind] shall flow rivers of living water' (John 7.37–38).

Next Enoch saw how the Man was given the Name before sun and stars were made; in other words, he saw how a human figure was named as Yahweh in the holy of holies that represented the state before and beyond the material creation. This was *theosis*, and this Chosen One became the source of *wisdom, understanding and knowledge*.[66] Isaiah had learned that the punishment for those who had rejected Wisdom was the loss of understanding and knowledge (Isa. 6.10), and that this would be restored through the Anointed One with his gifts of, among other things, *wisdom, understanding and knowledge* (Isa. 11.2). The Proverbs of Solomon were to give knowledge of *wisdom, instruction and understanding* (Prov. 1.2), but we best glimpse the older Wisdom in the Priestly writer's description of Bezalel, the designer and contractor for the desert tabernacle. The LORD filled him with a spirit of the *'elohim*, with *wisdom, understanding, knowledge* and 'craftsmanship', *mᵉla'ka'*. This latter is an interesting word, being the feminine form of the word 'angel', and so suggesting that craftsmanship was the partner or reciprocal of the angel. The wisdom of the *'elohim* is better translated 'the wisdom of the angels/heavenly beings' than 'the wisdom of God'.

Water, that is, Wisdom, streaming from the throne and the holy of holies was a recurring theme in the Hebrew scriptures, but the expectation changed. For the psalmist it was a present hope:

> The children of men take refuge in the shadow of thy wings.
> They feast on the abundance of thy house,
> And thou givest them drink from the river of thy delights.
> For with thee is the fountain of life;
> In thy light do we see light.   (Ps. 36.7–9)

This may be the river whose streams 'make glad the city of God' (Ps. 46.4), of which Isaiah spoke when he said that the righteous would

---

[66] *1 Enoch* 49.1–3.

see the king in his beauty and majesty, in a place with broad rivers and streams on each side (Isa. 33.15, 17, 21).

Jeremiah knew of a change and lamented that his people had rejected the fountain of living water:

> A glorious throne set on high from the beginning
> Is the place of our sanctuary.
> [But] ... they have forsaken the LORD
> The fountain of living water.
>
> (Jer. 17.12–13, also 2.12–13)[67]

For the prophets it became a future hope, for the time of the Messiah:

> ... the earth shall be full of the knowledge of the LORD
> As the waters cover the sea.   (Isa. 11.9; Hab. 2.14)

> On that day living waters shall flow out from Jerusalem ...
> And the LORD will become king over all the earth.
>
> (Zech. 14.8–9; also Joel 3.18; Ezek. 47.1–12)

And for the 'new' Wisdom teachers it became just a proverb:

> The teaching of the wise is a fountain of life ...   (Prov. 13.14)

> The fear of the LORD is a fountain of life ...   (Prov. 14.27)

Similar imagery is found in the Qumran Hymns, which describe the life of the community in a desert place; this may be a literal description of their home, but it was more than that. They had been living in a spiritual desert but had rediscovered the spring, fountain and river that 'Ezra' withheld from the public canon of Scripture. They sang of 'the eternal [spring], the well of glory, and the fountain of knowledge';[68] 'A source of light that becomes a flowing eternal fountain'[69] and in this they put their trust; 'My heart shall be open to the everlasting fountain; my support shall be in the strength from on high.'[70] And they gave thanks to the LORD:

> You have set me by a source of streams in a dry land,
> By a spring of water in a desert ...

---

[67] And also *1 Enoch* 96.6.
[68] 1QH XX.29. Brackets thus [***] indicate an uncertain piece of text.
[69] 1QH XIV.17.
[70] 1QH XVIII.32; 'heart' means 'mind'.

> Trees of life by a spring of mystery, *raz*,
> They had not yet caused (it) to bud,
> But they sent out their roots to the watercourse,
> And the stem was opened to the living waters
> And it was like an eternal fountain.[71]

The poem continues with tree of life imagery: mighty ones, spirits of holiness and whirling flames of fire prevent access to the fruit of the tree; and nobody could approach the 'well-spring of life' or drink the 'holy waters' unless he discerned and believed in the fountain of life. All this is Eden imagery; the curse on Adam and Eve had been removed so they had access again to the tree of life (Gen. 3.22–24), just as Jesus promised the faithful Christian: 'To him who conquers I will grant to eat of the tree of life, which is in the paradise of God' (Rev. 2.7, cf. 22.14). The teacher, *maśkil*, in the Qumran community listened to the secret council by means of the holy Spirit: 'In the mystery of your wisdom you have opened knowledge to me, And in your mercies you have opened for me the fountain of your might.' They said of him: 'You placed (understanding) in his heart/mind to open the source of knowledge for those who discern.'[72] John described the same experience; he was in the Spirit on the day of the LORD (Rev. 1.10), and then received revelations.

The *Community Rule* set these hymns in their context, which was the holy of holies.

> My eyes have looked at eternal things,
> which are hidden from a man,
> knowledge and prudence
> [hidden] from the sons of Adam,
> a spring of righteousness, a store of strength,
>   with a fountain of glory,
> [hidden] from the assembly of the flesh.

All this had been given to the community, described as the chosen ones, the holy ones, who had been joined to the assembly of the sons of heaven.[73] They were angels on earth.

The Qumran Wisdom texts had some things in common with the biblical Wisdom texts, such as advice about daily living: 'Do not sell

---

[71] 1QH XVI.5–8.

[72] 1QH XX.14–15; 1QH X.20.

[73] *Community Rule*, 1QSa XI.6–7.

yourself for money', or 'Do not count a man of iniquity as your helper'.[74] But there was other material that set this Wisdom teaching in a wider context; not as the secular wise sayings of the ancient royal courts that enabled young men to succeed in life, but as knowledge of the eternal truths that enabled the initiate to live in harmony with the creation and know the divine secrets. This was the knowledge revealed by angels that we glimpsed in Tobit. In the Qumran texts, advice to a poor person was set alongside the exhortation to study the *raz nihyeh*, the mystery of existence (if that is how to translate the words), so that he could understand the divine plan.[75] This was nothing new; the psalmist had pondered the problem of evil people, but only received an answer when he went into the sanctuary of God, and there he perceived what would happen afterwards (Ps. 73.17). So too with Second-Isaiah, when the LORD reminded him what he had been taught 'from the beginning . . . from the foundations of the earth' (Isa. 40.21). The prophet had stood in the holy of holies, the source of creation, whence he could look out and see all history. John was summoned to stand before the throne, to be shown 'what must take place after this' (Rev. 4.1).

The *raz nihyeh* involved, among other things, the link between the pattern of creation, human conduct and the day of judgement. A tentative reconstruction of the great Qumran Wisdom text[76] suggests that the teaching was set in 'a cosmic and eschatological theological framework' and the instruction enabled a person to 'align himself with the correct order of the cosmos'.[77] Isaiah's Servant, who was also a *maśkil* (Isa. 52.13),[78] was high and lifted up and became wise and understanding. He made many righteous by his knowledge. In other words, his knowledge put people back into harmony with God's plan – which is what righteousness means (Isa. 53.11). We shall return to this later, but suffice it here to note that this was the subject of the great hymn in heaven when the seventh angel blew the last trumpet: the kingdom was established on earth, the servants and saints of the LORD were rewarded, but

---

[74] 4Q416 and 4Q417.

[75] Thus 4Q416.

[76] 4Q416.

[77] D. J. Harrington, *Wisdom Texts from Qumran*, London: Routledge, 1996, p. 41.

[78] This verse has the verb, the Qumran hymn has the derived noun.

the dead were judged and the destroyers of creation were destroyed (Rev. 11.15–18).

The phrase *raz nihyeh* is found many times in the Qumran texts, and the fact that we cannot even translate the words with confidence, let alone explain what they mean, is an indication of how little is known of their matrix in temple and wisdom. The Qumran community criticized some contemporaries because they did not know what they were talking about: 'For it has been sealed up from you. Sealed is the vision, and on the eternal mysteries you have not looked, and you have not come to understand knowledge.'[79] Early Christian writers said much the same, and spoke of the temple tradition as the mysteries. This did not mean that they were drawn from or modelled on the various contemporary mystery cults; it meant only that they were using the same language and therefore had to use the same Greek words. Bishop Ignatius of Antioch, in the second or third generation, emphasized the need for unity among his flock and for the true teaching, which included rather more than we find in the New Testament. He understood 'celestial secrets and angelic hierarchies and the dispositions of the heavenly powers and much else both seen and unseen . . .', yet this alone did not make him a disciple.[80] He reminded his people: 'You are initiates of the same mysteries as our saintly and renowned Paul',[81] but his 'mysteries' were compared to those of the ancient temple priests:

> The priests of old, I admit, were estimable men, but our own High Priest is greater, for he has been entrusted with the Holy of Holies. And to him alone are the secret things of God committed. He is the doorway to the Father, and it is by him that Abraham and Isaac and Jacob and the prophets go in, no less than the apostles and the whole Church; for all these have their part in God's unity.[82]

Clement of Alexandria is often said to have been adopting contemporary Greek ideas, but he too was writing about temple mysticism. Paul, he taught, clearly revealed that some knowledge was not given to everyone, 'for there were certainly among the Hebrews some things

---

[79] *The Book of Mysteries*, 4Q300.
[80] Ignatius, *To the Trallians* 5.
[81] Ignatius, *To the Ephesians* 12.
[82] Ignatius, *To the Philadelphians* 9.

delivered unwritten . . .'[83] The goal of the Christian was to know these things and to behold them. This gave knowledge of past, present and future, and was Clement's way of describing the vision of God and the knowledge that this brought. 'As the Hebrews gazed on the glory of Moses and the prophets of Israel on the vision of angels, so we also become able to look the splendours of truth in the face.'[84] The person who attained the vision was transformed by it into a heavenly being. 'In this way it is possible for the Gnostic [the one who knows] already to have become God: "I said ye are gods and sons of the Highest."'[85]

Origen knew that temple teaching had been concealed from all but the high priests, and that much of the teaching was transmitted through liturgy rather than scripture. Much of the New Testament, e.g. Paul's letters, were sent to clarify certain points or as part of a dispute; they do not give a full picture of early Christian belief. So too with the Councils of the Church; the liturgies are better evidence of what Christians actually believed. Origen compared certain customs – praying towards the east, baptism rites, words used in the Eucharist – to the secrets of the holy of holies. The Levites who carried the tabernacle through the desert, as we have seen, were not permitted to look at what they were carrying. The high priests had to wrap all the sacred furnishings and vessels, before the Levites could lift them: 'they must not touch the holy things, lest they die' (Num. 4.15). Even the Levites did not fully understand what they were transmitting, yet according to the Ezra tradition, it was the Levites who explained the scriptures to the people.

If we take as our norm the 'Ezra' canon and interpretation and the Deuteronomists' account of temple worship – the usual practice – there is little evidence for temple mysticism. The Deuteronomists' description of the temple in 1 Kings 6—8 mentions neither the chariot throne nor the veil, but the Chronicler does (1 Chron. 28.18; 2 Chron. 3.14). Nor do the Deuteronomists mention temple music, even though the Chronicler makes music the most important part of the cult, with temple musicians established even before the temple itself (1 Chron. 16.1–6). The Chronicler also attributes to David a

[83] Clement, *Miscellanies* 5.10.
[84] Clement, *Miscellanies* 6.15.
[85] Clement, *Miscellanies* 4.23.

prayer in which he thanks the Lord for something that is now unreadable. A possible reconstruction is 'You caused me to see in the midst [or in a vision] the Man on high [or the Man ascending]' (1 Chron. 17.17). This is the figure we shall meet many times in our quest for temple mysticism: he is Adam before he sinned, he is Isaiah's Servant, high and lifted up, he is Daniel's Man ascending on the clouds of heaven (Dan. 7.13), he is the unnamed figure who ascends to heaven to acquire understanding, wisdom and knowledge (Prov. 30.1–4, another damaged text), and he is the one of whom John the Baptist said, 'He comes from heaven . . . [and] bears witness to what he has seen and heard' (John 3.31–32).

2

The One

Temple mystics entered the holy of holies and lived in that world. Entering the holy of holies meant returning to Day One and to the source of life, approaching the unity of the pre-created light and being transformed by the light into that light. R. Ishmael, a mystic of high priestly descent and a younger contemporary of John,[1] received a vision of the LORD enthroned when he was offering incense in the holy of holies.[2] He cannot have been literally in the temple as he was only a child when the temple was destroyed, but a saying attributed to him sums up the experience of the temple mystic:

> Ishma'el/he said: When my ears heard this great mystery,
> The world was changed around me into a shining place
> and my heart was as if I/it had come to a new world,
> and every day it seemed to my soul
> as though I was standing before the throne of glory.[3]

The mystics saw the world from the holy of holies; they saw it whole and because they looked with new eyes, they saw it differently. Since the holy of holies, as we shall see, was the kingdom, it was the kingdom perspective on the world. These high priestly figures were known by many names: they were the servants, they were the sons and they were the angels. This plurality within Day One, human access to Day One and the resulting transformation from the human state into the divine, known later as *theosis*, were all characteristic of Christianity, but, to judge from pre-Christian Jewish texts, they had all been controversial for some time before the advent of Christianity.

John presented Christianity as temple mysticism, but it was no longer necessary literally to enter the holy of holies to see the LORD

---

[1] R. Ishmael taught in Palestine in the early second century CE.
[2] Babylonian Talmud *Berakoth* 7a.
[3] *Merkavah Rabbah* 680, Schäfer's numbering. This is the gist of three almost parallel texts.

and the light, because the LORD and the light had come into the world. 'The true light that enlightens every man was coming into the world . . . [and] we have beheld his glory' (John 1.9, 14). When John described Jesus exhorting his disciples to believe in the light and so become sons of light (John 12.36), he immediately wrote of Isaiah's experience as a temple mystic – seeing the LORD in glory enthroned in the holy of holies. He described the Christian life as walking in the light, having passed already from death into life (1 John 1.7; 3.14).

The temple mystic learned the *raz nihyeh*, the mystery of life coming from the One, and by entering the holy of holies both literally and in his way of thinking, he recovered that unity. He was changed, and his way of seeing the world was changed. This was sometimes described as receiving wisdom or as acquiring a new way of knowing. Read John's familiar words in the context of temple mysticism:

> That which was from the beginning [the holy of holies], which we have heard, which we have seen with our eyes, which we have looked upon and touched with our hands, concerning the word of life – the life was made manifest, and we saw it, and testify to it, and proclaim to you the eternal life which was with the Father and was made manifest to us – that which we have seen and heard we proclaim also to you, so that you may have fellowship [unity] with us; and our fellowship [unity] is with the Father and with his Son Jesus Christ.
>
> (1 John 1.1–3)

Later in the letter he introduced other characteristic themes: the temple mystic acquired knowledge when he was anointed, and John wrote: 'But you have been anointed by the Holy One and you know all things' (or 'you all know') (1 John 2.20).

Temple mysticism had much in common with the mystery religions of the ancient world. This is not to suggest in any way that second temple Judaism adopted the newly fashionable Greek mystery cults of the Hellenistic period, but rather to put the first temple in its historical and cultural context. The religions of ancient Anatolia and Egypt had elements of 'mystery' cults, but most of the evidence for them is only found in much later Greek and Latin texts. Little that is certain can be known of them. Nobody knows the age of the most famous of the Greek mysteries at Eleusis, and the whole quest is hampered by the fact that initiates never revealed what they knew. The mysteries that flourished in the Mediterranean world from about 300 BCE, of which we are better informed, drew elements not only from Greece, but also from Anatolia, Egypt, Persia and Syria, and so it is impossible to generalize or identify sources with confidence.

The mysteries did, however, have certain characteristics relevant to our quest for temple mysticism, but most of the 'temple' texts are much older than the Greek or Latin material from which the Mediterranean mysteries are reconstructed. The highest state for the Eleusinian mysteries, for example, was 'beholding', but there is no way that Psalm 17 was influenced by alien mystery cults. After his suffering, the psalmist knew that he would see the LORD:

> I shall behold thy face in righteousness,
> When I awake I shall be satisfied with seeing thy form.
> (Ps. 17.15, my translation)

This was the state achieved by an initiate of the mysteries, but also by Isaiah's Suffering Servant, according to the oldest known Hebrew texts: 'After the suffering of his soul he will see light and be satisfied with his knowledge' (Isa. 53.11, translating the Qumran text literally). This passage is thought to come from the First-Isaiah before 700 BCE, re-used by a later disciple. The high priestly blessing, 'May the LORD make his face to shine upon you' (Num. 6.25), has been found on minute silver scrolls dated to about 600 BCE, the end of the first temple period.[4] One of the identifying characteristics of a mystery religion, then, was established in the temple before 700 BCE. It may be that the similarity to later mystery cults was a factor that led to the suppression of this aspect of the ancient temple.

The Greek mysteries involved sacred words spoken, *legomena*, sacred objects shown, *deiknumena*, and sacred acts done, *drōmena*,[5] and we recall that only the high priests were allowed to see the sacred furnishings of the tabernacle. Origen knew that the sacred objects represented the teaching and he implied that only the high priests learned this: 'If one is a priest to whom the sacred vessels, that is, the

---

[4] The Ketef Hinnom silver scrolls were found in the Valley of Hinnom. The inscription is not complete but 'LORD' and 'shine' are clear.

[5] See M. W. Meyer, *The Ancient Mysteries*, San Francisco: HarperSanFrancisco, 1987, p. 18.

secrets of mysterious Wisdom, have been entrusted, he must keep them veiled and not produce them easily for the people.'[6] So too Bishop Basil of Caesarea, writing in Cappadocia in the mid-fourth century CE. He (and others) used the language of the mysteries when writing about the sacraments and about the traditions of the Church for which there is no obvious scriptural source. After comparing the Apostles and Fathers of the Church to the ancient high priests who had exclusive access to the holy of holies, he wrote: '[They] used to preserve the sacred dignity of the mysteries in secrecy and silence';[7] 'The unwritten traditions are so many and they possess so great a strength for the mystery of our religion.'[8] He listed some of these as facing east to pray, signing with the cross at baptism, anointing with consecrated oil, and the words of *epiclesis* at the Eucharist. These correspond well with the sacred words, sacred objects and sacred acts that characterized the mysteries, but the early Christians knew that their mysteries had come from the temple. It is interesting that the leader of the Qumran community, the *m^ebaqqer*, a name that could accurately be translated as 'bishop', had to instruct his people in 'the things of eternity and their interpretation'[9] and, since the holy of holies represented eternity, he must have been instructing them in the mysteries.

The mystery religions usually had a sacred meal, representing a meal with the gods, and again, there is evidence for this in the oldest Hebrew texts. When the elders of Israel ascended Sinai 'they beheld God, and ate and drank' (Exod. 24.11), something the Deuteronomists denied. This meal after the vision has never been explained, nor the golden table in the tabernacle/temple on which were 'plates and dishes for incense, flagons and bowls with which to pour libations, [and] the bread of the Face/Presence' (Exod. 25.29–30). The bread was only for the high priests, to be eaten in the holy place (Lev. 24.5–9), and it was their most holy food. It imparted holiness.

We shall look now at three fundamental characteristics of temple mysticism: first, the unity, then the light and the glory.

---

[6] Origen, Homily 4, *On Numbers*.
[7] Basil, *On the Holy Spirit* 66.
[8] Basil, *On the Holy Spirit* 67.
[9] *Damascus Document* CD XIII.

Day One

The holy of holies appears briefly in Genesis 1 as Day One. Most English versions have 'the first day', but this is not correct. The Hebrew is 'one', and the Greek translation kept the curious usage. There must have been a reason for it. The other days of creation are 'in time' and so follow as the second day, the third day and so on. Day One meant that it was outside the temporal sequence of the material creation. It was not 'the first day' but the state beyond the temporal and material world; it was the eternal present. Just as the holy of holies was in the midst of the temple, so too the eternal presence of God was in the midst of creation. This was the original reason for building the tabernacle to that particular pattern: 'Let them make me a holy place that I may dwell in their midst' (Exod. 25.8, my translation). The holy of holies behind the veil symbolized God in the midst of the creation.

The veil of the temple was woven from threads of four colours: red, blue and purple – which we assume were wool – and white linen. In the time of Jesus these four colours symbolized the four elements from which people at that time believed the material world was made: the red was fire, the blue was air, the purple was water (because the dye came from a sea shell) and the white was the earth. Josephus, who came from a high priestly family, revealed this, and so it is likely to be correct.[10] What we cannot know is the age of this symbolism, but the idea that something concealed or rather 'veiled' the divine presence is found in Job's description of the creation and so could be ancient: 'He enclosed the presence of the throne, he spread upon it his cloud' (Job 26.9, translating literally[11]). The meaning of the tabernacle/temple plan was that matter concealed the divine presence in the midst of creation. Those who passed through the veil, or saw through the veil, saw the divine light in their midst.

The holy of holies beyond the veil was a cube-shaped room lined with gold (1 Kings 6.20) which housed the huge *cherubim* that represented the throne of the LORD. Hezekiah prayed: 'O LORD of Hosts, God of Israel, who art enthroned above the cherubim . . .' (Isa. 37.16); and the psalmist sang: 'Thou who art enthroned upon the cherubim, shine forth . . .' (Ps. 80.1). Isaiah said he had seen the King, the LORD

---

[10] Josephus, *War* 5.212–13.

[11] Hebrew 'moon' and 'throne' are written in the same way, but pronounced differently.

of Hosts, enthroned in the holy of holies (Isa. 6.5), and the holy
of holies was his kingdom. This was one of the meanings of Jesus'
saying: 'The kingdom of God is in the midst of you' (Luke 17.21);
he was reminding the Pharisees of something they already knew. For
John, the kingdom was the heavenly city and he naturally described
it as a golden cube (Rev. 21.15–18). It needed neither sun nor moon
to give light, because its light was the glory of God (Rev. 21.23).

Elsewhere the holy of holies is described as 'the beginning', but
this must be understood as 'the origin' rather than 'the first of a
temporal sequence'. The holy of holies was outside time, and so those
who entered looked out from beyond time and saw history as a whole.
Isaiah had been told about the future 'from the beginning': 'Has it
not been told you from the beginning? Have you not understood
from the foundations of the earth?' (Isa. 40.21). Isaiah had entered
the very heart and origin of the creation, and there he had seen
the future. John began his Gospel 'In the beginning was the Word'
(John 1.1), but, again, this was not 'beginning' in the temporal sense.
This was the glory that the Son shared with the Father 'before the
world was made' (John 17.5).

Philo explained:

> [Moses] says that 'in the beginning God made the heaven and the
> earth,' taking 'beginning' not, as some think, in a chronological sense,
> for time was not there before there was a world. Time began either
> simultaneously with the world or after it.[12]

The state beyond time that the holy of holies represented was 'eternity',
'olam, a word implying continuous or indefinite existence, and derived
from the word meaning 'hidden'. Those who entered this hidden state
passed beyond time into the eternal state that was present in their
midst, and they could see all history, both past and future. When R.
Ishmael stood in heaven before the throne, the great angel Metatron
showed him the whole history of the world on the reverse of the veil:
'[Everything] whether done or to be done in the time to come, till the
end of time, were all printed on the curtain of the Omnipresent One';[13]
and when Jesus told people of his experiences in the wilderness, he
said that he had seen 'all the kingdoms of the world in a moment of

---

[12] Philo, *On the Creation* 26.
[13] *3 Enoch* 45.6.

time' (Luke 4.5). Luke also described Jesus' ascent into heaven in temple language: he blessed the disciples, they worshipped him, he was lifted up in a cloud, and two angels[14] appeared (Luke 24.50–51; Acts 1.9–11). Jesus the high priest was passing from the particular time and place of Bethany in the first century CE into the eternal present.

Even though Genesis was part of the open canon of scripture, the first verses were forbidden for public reading, presumably because they concerned Day One,[15] and the rabbis debated what Day One, or One Day, meant. According to R. Judan,[16] it was the state of divine unity underlying all creation: 'The day in which the Holy One, blessed be he, was One in his universe.'[17] Since Day One was without time or matter, there was no means of dividing it. The unity, though, was not the problem; it was the plurality within the undivided unity. Other texts imply that there were angels in Day One, before the material world was created, but the angels were a sensitive matter because they implied plurality. The rabbis could not agree when the angels were created but they did agree that it was not on Day One.[18]

There are, however, texts in the Hebrew scriptures that do imply the existence of angels on Day One and thus plurality within the divine. The word *'elohim*, usually translated 'God', is a plural form and could as easily be translated 'gods' or 'angels'. Psalm 82.1 illustrates the problem: *''elohim* has taken his place in the council of El, in the midst of *'elohim* he holds judgement'. The first is usually translated 'God' and the second 'gods'. In Genesis 1, creation is the work of *'elohim* ('God' or 'angels'?), and there are both singular and plural verbs: 'And *'elohim* said [sing.] "Let us make [pl.] ..."' (Gen. 1.26). The *Shema'* is also ambiguous: 'The LORD our *'elohim* is one LORD' (Deut. 6.4). This could mean that the LORD was a unity, just as Day One was a unity. The psalmist described the LORD's angels and ministers before he described the creation of land and sea (Ps. 104.4, 5), implying that they existed before the creation of land and sea, and Job knew of the morning stars and sons of God who sang as the LORD established the foundations of the earth (Job 38.4–7). They

---

[14] Men in white means angels.
[15] Mishnah *Ḥagigah* 2.1.
[16] Teaching in Palestine in the fourth century CE.
[17] *Genesis Rabbah* III.8.
[18] *Genesis Rabbah* I.3.

knew of angels in Day One. The full version of the Benedicite,[19] which describes the creation in order, begins by praising the One enthroned in the temple, upon the *cherubim*, in his kingdom and in heaven, and then lists all the non-material creation – angels, powers and weathers – before listing the earth and the visible creation as described in Genesis 1. The author of the Benedicite, and all those who sang it, knew of angels in Day One. The *Book of Jubilees* gives the clearest picture of how Moses watched the process of creation and saw first the creation of all the spirits that serve before the throne: angels of presence, angels of holiness, of winds and weathers 'and of all the spirits of his creatures which are in heaven and on earth'.[20]

The Deuteronomic school that was so influential in the writing and transmission of the Hebrew scriptures warned against these esoteric teachings. 'The secret things belong to the LORD our God; but the things that are revealed belong to us and to our children for ever, that we may do all the words of this Law' (Deut. 29.29). They did not deny that the secret things existed but they forbade any investigation, and it was their spiritual heirs who forbade the reading and explanation of certain passages of scripture and eventually decided to keep secret the books of wisdom, understanding and knowledge.[21] The Law was more readily available, they said. 'It is not in heaven, that you should say "Who will go up for us to heaven, and bring it to us, that we may hear it and do it?" Neither is it beyond the sea, that you should say, "Who will go over the sea for us, and bring it to us, that we may hear it and do it?"' (Deut. 30.12–13).

The Deuteronomists must have known people who ascended to heaven and crossed the sea (what sea?) to bring down teaching from heaven. An obscure (possibly obscured?) text in Proverbs belongs in this context, linking ascent into heaven to *understanding, wisdom and knowledge*: 'I have not the understanding of a man, I have not learned wisdom, nor have I the knowledge of the holy ones . . .' (Prov. 30.2b–3, my translation).[22] The psalmist had sung of the throne surrounded by waters, and presumably this was the sea that the seeker had to cross: 'The LORD sits enthroned over the flood; the LORD sits enthroned

---

[19] Part of the Greek version of Daniel, but not in the Hebrew text.
[20] *Jubilees* 2.2.
[21] See above, p. 16.
[22] We shall return to this and look at the entire passage in context. See below, pp. 155–6.

as king for ever' (Ps. 29.10). Since Psalm 29 is one of the oldest psalms, Isaiah would have known this temple imagery too, even though he does not mention any sea in his vision of the throne. Heaven for the first Christians was the holy of holies where the throne of God was surrounded by a crystal sea (Rev. 4.6). John saw the faithful standing on its shore (Rev. 15.2), and, according to a story known in the time of Jesus, the archangel Michael froze the sea so that Adam could walk over.[23] John saw the Lamb who went and took the scroll from the one seated on the throne (Rev. 5.7), so he must have crossed the sea, even though John does not mention it. People who crossed the sea to acquire heavenly teaching set themselves in a scene like that of the Lamb who received the scroll.

The elders of Israel saw the God of Israel in their vision on Sinai when the commandments were given (Exod. 24.9–11); Isaiah saw the LORD enthroned when he was called as a prophet (Isa. 6.1–5); Ezekiel saw the throne, and a human figure on the throne, leaving the temple and going to Babylon when he was called as a prophet (Ezek. 1.4–28; 10.1–22); and Daniel saw 'one like a son of man', that is, a human figure, approaching the fiery throne that was set over a great sea (Dan. 7.2–14). John, too, received his revelations from the throne.

There is an enigmatic line in Proverbs 29.18 that has prompted a whole variety of translations:

- 'Where there is no vision, the people perish' (AV).
- 'Where there is no prophecy the people cast off restraint' (RSV).
- 'A nation without God's guidance is a nation without order' (GNB).
- 'Where there is no one in authority, the people break loose' (NEB).
- 'Where there is no vision the people get out of hand' (JB).

The Hebrew, literally, is 'Where there is no prophetic vision, the people go loose/unravel'. It was the shared vision at the centre, Day One, that was the source of unity for the people to whom it had been granted.

Pythagoras

Evidence for temple mysticism in later, and especially in Christian texts, has often been identified as Platonism or Neoplatonism. Ancient

---

[23] *The Life of Adam and Eve* 29.3.

writers, however, knew that Plato had taken some of his ideas from Hebrew sources, and in particular that Pythagoras had learned much from the Jerusalem temple. At this stage it is necessary to look at some of the similarities and to establish who took from whom, since elements of temple mysticism could have survived outside Hebrew sources.

Pythagoras was a younger contemporary of Ezekiel, and Hermippus of Smyrna, a *Greek* writing in the mid-third century BCE, said that Pythagoras had adopted the teachings of the Jews. Josephus emphasized this in his debate with Apion, and quoted Hermippus: '[Pythagoras] imitated the doctrines of the Jews ... which he transferred into his own philosophy.'[24] Since Socrates' disciple Timaeus was a follower of Pythagoras, elements of ancient temple teaching and temple mysticism can be traced in the writings of Plato, and when this appears in, say, the writings of Philo, it is a mistake to identify it too readily as Platonism. Several ancient writers claimed that Pythagoras had learned from the Jews: Aristobulus, for example, a Jew writing in the mid-second century BCE, said that 'Pythagoras transferred many of our doctrines and integrated them into his own beliefs.'[25] Eusebius, a Christian bishop writing in the early fourth century CE, devoted a large section of his work *The Preparation of the Gospel*[26] to showing how much had passed from Hebrew teaching into Greek philosophy.

Pythagoras himself left no writings, but an account of his life, written much later, said that he travelled widely during his youth and spent some time in 'Syria', living near Mount Carmel before going on to Egypt. 'He was initiated into the sacred operations that are performed in many parts of Syria',[27] which sounds like initiation into a mystery religion. Since 'Syria' included Judea, the similarities between the teachings of Pythagoras and the secret lore of the temple priests are unlikely to be concidence. He would have been in 'Syria' in the mid-sixth century BCE, and so immediately after the destruction of

---

[24] Josephus, *Against Apion* 1.22. For more detail see my book *The Great High Priest*, London: T&T Clark, 2003, pp. 263–5.

[25] Quoted in Eusebius, *Preparation of the Gospel* 13.12.

[26] English translation of *Preparation of the Gospel* by E. H. Gifford, Oxford: Oxford University Press, 1903.

[27] Iamblichus, who died about 330 CE, *Life of Pythagoras*, tr. T. Taylor, London: Watkins, (1818), 1965, p. 7.

the first temple. Six centuries later, Josephus, who knew the Essenes well, said that they had the same lifestyle as the Pythagoreans,[28] and the writings from Qumran suggest the community there were a conservative priestly group. Scholars have been unable to identify what prompted Pythagoras' characteristic teachings and admit that his 'science' presupposed a mythological framework. Aristotle criticized the Pythagoreans for this approach: '[They] do not seek accounts and explanations in conformity with appearances, but try by violence to bring the appearances into line with accounts and opinions of their own.'[29] This 'myth' seems to have been the world view of the Jerusalem temple which corresponds to a remarkable degree with what is known of the teachings of Pythagoras.[30]

Plato's *Timaeus*, for example, has an account of the creation given by Timaeus, a Pythagorean. Bury summarized thus, and fell naturally into biblical language:

> The theme of that central Myth is nothing less than the Creation of the Universe ... We are transported in imagination to a point 'beyond the beginning of years' when time was not and 'the earth was without form and void'. There we follow, step by step, the process whereby the World was built up into a harmonious structure, and Cosmos evolved out of Chaos.[31]

This is the Greek version of the *raz nihyeh*, the mystery of how all things are, how life in its variety can spring from the eternal unity. 'In the beginning was the Word ... in him was life' is how this appears in the fourth Gospel, but Aristotle criticized the Pythagoreans for this teaching: 'It is strange also to attribute generation to eternal things, or rather, this is one of the things that are impossible.'[32]

There are several elements of Pythagorean lore and imagery that can only have come from temple teaching. They believed, for example, that there was a fire in the centre of the universe, something that has been described as 'one of the most vexed questions in the

---

[28] Josephus, *Antiquities* 15.371.

[29] Aristotle, *On the Heavens* 293A.

[30] For detail, see my book *The Great High Priest*, London: T&T Clark, 2003, pp. 262–93.

[31] *Plato in Twelve Volumes*, Loeb edition, Cambridge MA: Harvard University Press, (1929), 1989, vol. IX, tr. R. G. Bury, Introduction, pp. 3, 5.

[32] Artistotle, *Metaphysics* N3 1091a.

history of Greek philosophy'.[33] They believed that 'at the centre of the four elements there lies a certain unitary fiery cube'.[34] Now a unitary fiery cube sounds very like the holy of holies, and the four elements sounds like the veil that screened it. The gold that lined the holy of holies represented fire, and visionaries described it as a place of fire. Isaiah wrote of the upright person who could 'dwell with the devouring fire' and then 'see the king in his beauty' in 'a place of broad rivers and streams' (Isa. 33.14, 17, 21). The Qumran *Thanksgiving Hymns* resolved this difficulty of fire and water together by saying that the streams were fire or water, depending on the recipient:

> . . . and the spring of light
> Will become an eternal fountain that never fails
> And in its shining flames,
> all the sons of [ ] will burn
> As a fire burning up
> all the men who are guilty . . .[35]

When Ezekiel described the chariot throne leaving the temple, he was describing the holy of holies as he knew and imagined it: brightness, a fire flashing forth continually, and in the midst of the fire something like gleaming bronze. There was a fiery human figure on the throne, surrounded by a rainbow (Ezek. 1.4, 26–28). Daniel saw the Ancient of Days on a fiery throne above a stream of fire (Dan. 7.9–14). Enoch described the holy of holies as a fiery place, with floor and ceiling of fire where the Great Glory sat enthroned, with fire all around him. No angel was allowed to enter the holy of holies.[36] In another account, Enoch described the house of fire encircled by angels, which only the archangels could enter.[37] One of the Qumran *Sabbath Songs* shows how that community imagined the holy of holies in the time of Jesus:

> From between his glorious wheels there is as it were a fiery vision of most holy spirits. Above them is the appearance of rivulets of fire in the likeness of gleaming brass . . . radiance in many coloured glory . . .[38]

---

[33] Thus P. Kingsley, *Ancient Philosophy, Mystery and Magic. Empedocles and the Pythagorean Tradition*, Oxford: Clarendon, 1995, p. 172.

[34] Kingsley, *Ancient Philosophy, Mystery and Magic*, p. 183.

[35] *Thanksgiving Hymns*, 1QH XIV.20b, 21.

[36] *1 Enoch* 14.15–22.

[37] *1 Enoch* 71.1–11.

[38] *Sabbath Songs*, 4Q405.

The Pythagoreans also described the central fiery cube as Zeus' tower or the throne of Zeus.[39] The holy of holies as the throne needs no further illustration, but the holy of holies as a tower is less well known. Isaiah's watchtower in the middle of the vineyard (Isa. 5.2) was understood to be the holy of holies,[40] and this is where Habakkuk took his place when he was waiting for a vision of the future: 'I will take my stand to watch, and station myself on the tower, and look forth to see what he will say to me' (Hab. 2.1). Enoch was taken up onto a tower to watch the history of his people unfold before him.[41] When the apostate generation who returned from Babylon rebuilt the temple, Enoch said they 'raised up the tower' and set a table before it, meaning they rebuilt the holy of holies and set out the table for the shewbread.[42] And it was from this tower that the LORD looked out:

> The LORD looks out from heaven.
> He sees all the children of men;
> From where he sits enthroned he looks forth
> On all the inhabitants of the earth.
>
> (Ps. 33.13, my translation)

Some translations have 'looks down' from heaven, but this is not implied in the Hebrew; the LORD looks *out* from the holy of holies.

Plato described the fiery cube as the place where Zeus gathered the gods together: 'He gathered all the gods together in their most honourable home which stands at the centre of the universe and watches over everything that belongs to the world of becoming.'[43] This is unmistakable as the holy of holies, where the LORD of Hosts was enthroned amid the hosts (e.g. Rev. 5.11). The Pythagoreans also identified this fiery centre as the present moment, and as the number one,[44] and they described unity as 'the chariot'.[45] Unity as a chariot must have been a memory of the chariot throne in the temple, and

---

[39] Kingsley, *Ancient Philosophy, Mystery and Magic*, n. 33 above, pp. 187, 195.

[40] Thus R. Yosi, in the early second century CE, Tosefta *Sukkah* 3.15: 'He built a tower in the midst of it . . . This is the sanctuary.'

[41] *1 Enoch* 87.4.

[42] *1 Enoch* 89.73.

[43] Plato, *Critias* 121C.

[44] Kingsley, *Ancient Philosophy, Mystery and Magic*, p. 183.

[45] Iamblichus, *Theologoumena Arithmeticae* 6, ed. V. de Falco, Leipzig: Teubneri, 1922.

the holy of holies was the eternal present. We shall return many times to Pythagoras and Plato, to reclaim temple teachings.

The light

'May the LORD make his face to shine on you' (Num. 6.25) was the high priestly blessing, but it was also a forbidden text. Some Targums did not translate it into Aramaic, and it was not to be explained.[46] Why?

'Seeing' the LORD and his shining face had various meanings. In the sagas and early histories the LORD shut Noah into the ark (Gen. 7.16) and came to look at the tower of Babel (Gen. 11.5). This was, perhaps, just the storyteller's anthropomorphic turn of phrase. Then there were visions and dreams (e.g. Gen. 15.1; 28.12–15), but there were also 'appearances' (e.g. Gen. 12.7; 17.1), and even appearances where the LORD seems to be one of three men at Mamre (Gen. 18.1–2).[47] The elders saw the God of Israel at Sinai (Exod. 24.10), and the LORD said he would appear to Aaron over the mercy seat (Lev. 16.2). Isaiah saw the LORD enthroned in the temple, and Ezekiel saw him leave, but then Deuteronomy denied that the LORD had been seen when the commandments were given (Deut. 4.12). After this point, 'seeing' the LORD became a sensitive matter, and circumlocutions were found. The 'vision' was denied by the very people who warned against the secret things and emphasized instead that the Law was sufficient (Deut. 29.29). This change affected the subsequent transmission of older texts and, as a result, the way they have been read.

The influence of the Deuteronomists and their heirs can be detected in several places. Two other examples must suffice to illustrate the point. Their calendar does not mention the day of atonement (Deut. 16, cf. Lev. 23), and their hand is clear in the final arrangement of the book of Exodus. Deuteronomy 9—10 summarizes their story of the second law, which is what the name Deuteronomy means. The first tablets of the Law were broken because Aaron led the people astray with the golden calf, and Moses was given the second set of tablets (Deut. 10.1–5). The fuller version of the story in Exodus reveals

---

[46] Mishnah *Megillah* 4.10. Some versions say the blessing was not even read out.

[47] But see also below, p. 66.

the changes that the Deuteronomists introduced, along with the 'second law'. First, Moses wanted to offer himself as atonement for the people's sin – he must have thought that this was possible – and the LORD then revealed that each person was responsible for his own sin: 'Whoever has sinned against me, him will I blot out of my book' (Exod. 32.33). One person making atonement for another was not possible. This explains the omission from the Deuteronomists' calendar.

Immediately after this, Moses, who spoke with the LORD face to face (Exod. 33.11), asked to see the glory of the LORD (Exod. 33.18). Some older material in Numbers, traditionally assigned to the early period of the first temple, describes Moses as the servant of the LORD who saw the form, *t^emunah*, of the LORD (Num. 12.8); and the psalmist, in the same period, was confident that his prayer would be heard: 'I shall behold, *hazah*,[48] thy face in righteousness, when I awake I shall be satisfied with thy form, *t^emunah*' (Ps. 17.15). In Greek, this became: 'I shall be satisfied by seeing your glory.' From the parallelism of Hebrew poetry, we deduce that 'form' and 'face' were equivalent terms, and that the 'form' was understood as the 'glory'. When the Moses of the older tradition asked to see the glory, he was asking to see the face or the form. But the story changed.

When the Deuteronomists edited the story, Moses asked to see the glory (Exod. 33.18), but the LORD said that he would reveal only his Name 'but . . . you cannot see my face; for man shall not see me and live' (Exod. 33.20). Moses was then hidden in a cleft of the rock while the glory passed by: 'You shall see my back; but my face shall not be seen' (Exod. 33.23). The Deuteronomists had emphasized that when the commandments were given, 'The LORD spoke to you out of the midst of the fire; you heard the sound of words, but saw no form, *t^emunah*; there was only a voice' (Deut. 4.12). Similarly, it was not the LORD who dwelt in the temple, but his Name. Nobody knows what was meant by this, but it was a mark of the Deuteronomists: 'You shall seek the place which the LORD your God will choose . . . to put his name . . .' (Deut. 12.5). Similarly, in the prayer they put into the mouth of Solomon when the temple was consecrated: 'Behold, heaven and the highest heaven cannot contain thee; how much

---

[48] This verb implies seeing in a vision.

less this house which I have built ... This house, the place of which thou hast said "My name shall be there" ...' (1 Kings 8.27, 29). The Deuteronomists and their heirs warned against the secret things, denied that atonement was possible, and denied that the 'form' of the LORD was ever seen, yet these were all fundamentals of the older temple cult.

In the Hebrew scriptures, then, there are two positions: the LORD could be seen – the temple tradition – and the LORD could not be seen. 'We have beheld his glory' wrote John (John 1.14), and the climax of the book of Revelation, and thus of the New Testament, is that servants of God-and-the-Lamb[49] stand before his throne and see his face (Rev. 22.4). Christianity was rooted in the older temple tradition and its mysticism.

The pilgrims to the original temple in Jerusalem came to see the face/presence[50] of the LORD, or so the older Hebrew scriptures said, but the correcting scribes changed the way those words had to be read. In the present text we read that three times a year – at the feast of Unleavened Bread, at the feast of Weeks and at the feast of Tabernacles – all the men of Israel had to 'appear before the LORD', but the text had been 'see the face of the LORD' (Exod. 23.17; 34.23; Deut. 16.16).[51] This does not require any change in the consonants, just different vowels, which were not written in the text anyway until well into the Christian era. At some stage the original pronunciation was changed, even though the resulting Hebrew was awkward. The Hebrew Lexicon says that all these passages were altered 'to avoid the expression "see the face of the LORD"'.[52]

The Psalms show that the shining face of the LORD was central to temple worship, even though we do not know exactly what this meant – how it was represented in ritual, for example. For Isaiah and Ezekiel it was a visionary experience, but there must have been something else for the pilgrims. Some have suggested that it was the sunrise shining directly into the temple at the great festivals which fell at the spring (Passover) and autumn (Tabernacles) equinoxes;

---

[49] God-and-the-Lamb indicates the twofold nature of the One enthroned, see below p. 104.

[50] In Hebrew, 'face' and 'presence' are the same word.

[51] Other examples: Exodus 23.15; 34.20; 34.24: Deuteronomy 31.11; 1 Samuel 1.22; Isaiah 1.12.

[52] F. Brown, R. Driver, C. Briggs, *A Hebrew and English Lexicon of the Old Testament*, Oxford: Clarendon Press, 1962 edn, pp. 816, 908.

others that it was the appearance in glorious vestments of the king/ high priest who represented the presence of the LORD – Immanuel. Or it could have been the sun shining on the golden signet of the Name that the high priest wore on his turban.[53] The fact that we do not know about something so central to worship in the temple is an indication of how much has been lost.

The most familiar word that has survived from temple worship is Hallelu-jah, usually translated 'Praise the LORD', and it occurs either at the beginning or at the end of a psalm.[54] The Hebrew word *hll* can mean praise, but it also means shine, and, given the importance of the shining face/presence, it may have meant 'Shine, LORD'. Perhaps Psalm 22.23 – 'praise him ... glorify him ... stand in awe of him ...' – should be *'make him shine* ... make him glorious ... stand in awe of him ...'[55] The duty of the Levites would have been 'to invoke, to thank and *to make the LORD shine ...'* (1 Chron. 16.4), and when they did this, 'the house of the LORD was filled with a cloud ... for the glory of the LORD filled the house' (2 Chron. 5.13–14). The music brought the glory of the LORD to the temple. The Deuteronomists never mentioned the music when the temple was consecrated; the glory came when the ark was set in place (1 Kings 8.6–11).

The shining face/presence of the LORD is a frequent theme in the Psalms. 'I shall behold thy face' (Ps. 17.15); 'Thy face, LORD, do I seek' (Ps. 27.8); 'Let thy face/presence shine on thy servant' (Ps. 31.16); 'Out of Zion ... God shines forth' (Ps. 50.2); 'May God ... make his face/presence shine upon us' (Ps. 67.1); 'Let your face/presence shine and we shall be saved' (Ps. 80.3). There are many examples. Seeing the light meant security: 'The LORD is my light and my salvation; whom shall I fear?' (Ps. 27.1); but if the LORD hid his face, it meant disaster: 'Thou didst hide thy face, I was dismayed' (Ps. 30.7). The Targum of Psalms, reflecting later sensitivities, never had simply 'the face' of the LORD appearing in the temple. Frequently 'face'

---

[53] The *Infancy Gospel of James* tells the story of Joachim, the father of Mary, who went to the temple to see if his sins were forgiven. He knew he would receive his answer by looking at the golden plate on the high priest's forehead.

[54] The exception is Psalm 135.3.

[55] There is a curious confirmation of this meaning centuries later, in an explanation of the liturgy by Germanus, Patriarch of Constantinople 715–730 CE. He said that Allelouia meant 'Our God will come clearly/visibly and fire shall go before him' (*On the Divine Liturgy*, 29). He knew that 'Allelouia' meant theophany.

was replaced by the Shekinah, the indwelling presence, or by other circumlocutions. Thus, for example, the Targums of Psalm 27.8 and 30.7 had Shekinah; the Targum of Psalm 17.15 became 'the glory of the face'; the Targum of Psalm 31.16 became 'the brightness' of the face; the Targum of Psalm 67.1 became 'the splendour' of the face.

The old calendars linked seeing the face to the temple pilgrimages, but an ancient poem known as the *Blessing of Moses* suggests that this 'shining' was particularly linked to the time when the LORD became King.

> The LORD came from Sinai
> And dawned from Seir upon us
> He shone forth from Mount Paran,
> He came with ten thousands of holy ones
> With [******] at his right hand ...
> Thus the LORD became king ...
> (Deut. 33.2, 5)

The missing words, usually translated 'flaming fire', are yet more evidence for the work of the correcting scribes. The original was probably the name of the Queen Mother in the temple, Ashratah, who was symbolized by the throne and by a shining cloud.[56]

The LORD became King at Tabernacles, and in the second temple period the memory of the original temple, as depicted in the *Blessing of Moses*, became the future hope. This can be seen in the collection of oracles in Zechariah 14.5b–9, translating the difficult Hebrew literally.

> 5b. 'Then the LORD my God will come [and] all the holy ones with you/him.'
> 6. 'On that day there shall be neither cold nor frost' is a damaged text, and the original was probably 'On that day there shall be no light, and the glorious ones shall dwindle', i.e. the heavenly bodies would lose their light.[57]
> 7. 'It will be Day One. This is known to the LORD. There shall be no day and no night and there shall be light at evening time.'
> 8. 'On that day living waters shall flow out of Jerusalem ...'
> 9. 'And the LORD will become king over the whole land, and the LORD will be One and his Name will be One.'

---

[56] See below, p. 58.
[57] Thus Brown, Driver and Briggs, *Hebrew and English Lexicon*, p. 891.

In other words, when the King/kingdom appeared, it was Day One, the lights of heaven were no longer needed, water/wisdom flowed from Jerusalem, and the LORD was One.[58]

The best known 'shining forth' of the presence of the LORD was the Transfiguration. Jesus told his disciples that before they died, some of them would see the Son of Man coming in his kingdom/the kingdom of God come with power/the kingdom of God (Matt. 16.28; Mark 9.1; Luke 9.27). Then, six days later,[59] he took Peter, James and John onto a mountain to pray and was transfigured. His garments (and his face, thus Matthew and Luke) shone, and he was talking to Moses and Elijah, the two men who had encountered the LORD on Sinai.[60] Peter wanted to make three tabernacles. Then a cloud (Matthew: 'a bright cloud') overshadowed them, and a voice said, 'This is my beloved/chosen Son. Listen to him.' What the disciples experienced on the mountain was the kingdom of God. The context – in Peter's mind at least – was Tabernacles, the time when, in the original temple, the LORD had become King and shone forth, presumably through the veil, or when the veil was drawn back.[61]

Now the kingdom was the holy of holies, but revealed only to a few. Jesus spoke of the secret of the kingdom, kept secret from outsiders by the parables (Mark 4.11). In the *Gospel of Thomas* there is a longer version of Jesus' saying 'the kingdom of God is in the midst of you' (Luke 17.21):

> The disciples said to him: 'When will the kingdom come?' [Jesus said] 'It will not come by waiting for it. It will not be a matter of saying "Here it is" or "There it is". The kingdom of the Father is spread out upon the earth and men do not see it.'[62]

This is the kingdom as the holy of holies; the ever-present presence, veiled by matter from many human eyes.

The Isaiah Targum, which includes material from the time of Jesus, shows that the kingdom was a revelation of the presence of the LORD:

---

[58] We shall return to this. See below, pp. 70–1.

[59] Eight days, according to Luke 9.28.

[60] In the Elijah story, the mountain is Horeb, but tradition fused the two.

[61] We shall return to this in the context of the Servant. See below, p. 151.

[62] *Gospel of Thomas* 113.

- 'The LORD of Hosts will reign on Mount Zion' (Isa. 24.23b) became 'the kingdom of the LORD of Hosts shall be revealed in the mountain of Zion' (Tg. Isa. 24.23b).
- 'The LORD of Hosts will descend to fight upon Mount Zion' (Isa. 31.4, my translation) became 'the kingdom of the LORD of Hosts will be revealed to dwell on Mount Zion' (Tg. Isa. 31.4).
- 'Your God reigns' (Isa. 52.7) became 'the kingdom of your God has been revealed' (Tg. Isa. 52.7).

In the Ezekiel Targum, the kingdom meant the judgement, as in Matthew's parable of the great catch of fish (Matt. 13.47–50), or John's vision of establishing the kingdom on earth (Rev. 11.15–18):

- 'Your doom has come to you, O inhabitant of the land' (Ezek. 7.7) became 'The kingdom has been revealed to you, O inhabitant of the land' (Tg. Ezek. 7.7).
- 'Your doom has come' (Ezek. 7.10) became 'The kingdom has been revealed' (Tg. Ezek. 7.10).

And we recall the cruel wordplay of the second-century Rabbis, that *evangelion*, gospel, means *aven gilyon*, worthless revelation, or *avon gilyon*, iniquitous revelation.[63]

In the time of Jesus the very name Israel was said to mean 'the man who sees God'.[64] Philo assumed this meaning many times in his works, e.g. 'for Israel means seeing God'.[65] The sons of Israel became, for him, 'the sons of the seeing one'.[66] This understanding of the name is doubtless linked to the way Exodus 25.8 was translated into Greek. Whereas the Hebrew has: 'Let them make me a sanctuary that I may dwell in their midst', the Greek is '. . . that I may be *seen* in their midst'. For the Greek-speaking Jews of Egypt, the LORD was *seen* in the holy of holies. This meaning – 'the man who sees God' – was adopted by most early Christian writers too. Hippolytus, writing in Rome in the early third century CE, applied the name Israel to Jesus: 'Having received then, all knowledge from the Father, the perfect Israel, the true Jacob, did show himself upon earth and conversed with men. And who is meant by Israel but a man who sees God?' He linked this

---

[63] See above, p. 20.

[64] Hebrew *'ish* = man, *ra'ah* = sees, *'el* = God.

[65] Philo, *Preliminary Studies* 51.

[66] Philo, *Allegorical Interpretation* III.15.

to John 1.14.[67] Eusebius too, a century later: 'Israel means the one who sees God in the manner of the knowing and perceiving mind.'[68]

'Seeing' God meant understanding, because with the vision came wisdom. This is apparent in the early Enoch material, where the priests' losing spiritual vision was equated with abandoning Wisdom: 'In the sixth week, all who live [in the temple] shall lose their sight, and their hearts shall godlessly forsake Wisdom.'[69] It is found in the Qumran *Thanksgiving Hymns*:

> You shine out to me in your strength . . .
> By me you have illumined the faces of many
> And you are strong beyond telling
> You have taught me your wonderful mysteries
>   and your wonderful counsel,
> And you have been my strength.[70]

and in some synagogue prayers that were adapted by the early Church:

> O God Almighty, the true God . . . who inhabitest light inaccessible . . .
> who art by nature invisible and yet art known to all reasonable natures
> who seek after thee with a good mind; the God of Israel, Thy people
> which truly see and which have believed in Christ . . .'[71]

Seeing the LORD brought understanding.

The priests blessed the Qumran community with an expanded version of the ancient blessing, showing how they understood the light of the Face: it meant illumination of the mind and a different way of knowing.

> May the LORD bless you and keep you
> *May he bless you with all good and keep you from all evil,*
>
> May the LORD make his face to shine on you and be gracious
>   to you
> *May he enlighten your mind with the insight/understanding*
>   *of life, may he be gracious to you with the knowledge of*
>   *eternity,*

---

[67] Hippolytus, *Against Noetus* 5.
[68] Eusebius, *Preparation of the Gospel* 11.6.
[69] *1 Enoch* 93.8.
[70] *Thanksgiving Hymns*, 1QH XII. 24b, 28–29a.
[71] *Apostolic Constitutions* 8.15.

May the LORD lift up his countenance upon you and give you
peace.
May he lift up his face upon you for eternal peace.[72]

Philo said that when the high priest was anointed, his mind was
'illuminated with a brilliant light',[73] and Justin described Christian
baptism in the same way: 'This washing is called illumination, because
they who learn these things are illuminated in their understanding.'[74]
He was not making an easy comparison with contemporary mystery
religions for the sake of his pagan reader; he was properly placing
baptism in its temple setting.

Philo said the same, using the language of the mystery religions,
when he was explaining the command to build a sanctuary: 'Make
me a sanctuary that I may be seen among you.' Seeing the LORD
altered the perception of everything else.

> If you are worthily initiated and can be consecrated to God and in
> a certain sense become a spiritual shrine of the Father, then instead
> of having closed eyes you will see the First [things?] and awakened
> you will cease from the deep sleep in which you have been held. Then
> there will appear to you that manifest One who causes incorporeal
> rays to shine for you and grants visions . . . For the beginning and the
> end of happiness is to be able to see God, but this cannot happen to
> him who has not made his soul a sanctuary and completely a shrine
> of God.[75]

Synesius, bishop of Ptolemais in Cyrene about 400 CE, explained
the difference between acquiring ordinary knowledge and what was
learned in the mysteries, referring to a writing of Aristotle that is
now lost:

> For the sacred matter [the contemplation achieved in the mysteries]
> is not like attention belonging to knowledge, or an outlet of mind . . .
> It is like Aristotle's view that men being initiated have not a lesson
> to learn but an experience to undergo and a condition into which
> they must be brought while they are becoming fit [to receive the
> revelation].[76]

---

[72] *Community Rule*, 1QS II.3.
[73] Philo, *On Flight* 110.
[74] Justin, *Apology* 1.61.
[75] Philo, *Questions on Exodus* II.51.
[76] Synesius, *Dio* 7.

This is exactly what Isaiah, our best witness to the mysticism of the first temple, said of the Anointed One:

> The Spirit of the LORD shall rest upon him . . .
> He shall not judge by what his eyes see,
> Or decide by what his ears hear . . .
> The earth shall be full of the knowledge of the LORD . . .
> (Isa. 11.2, 3, 9)

***

At the centre was the One, and the One was a Unity. The presence of the One was called the kingdom, and the temple mystics who entered the kingdom became part of the Unity, as Jesus prayed at the last supper: 'that they may be one, even as we are One . . . I desire that they also, whom thou hast given me, may be with me where I am, to behold my glory which thou hast given me in thy love for me before the foundation of the world' (John 17.11, 24). The presence of the One was also called the holy of holies, which did not mean 'very holy' but 'actively holy' or ' imparting holiness'. The temple mystics who entered the holy of holies became the holy ones, the saints, the angels. They extended the Unity because they were all part of it.

3

The Many

In order to explore how the Many related to the One, we look first at Dionysius, an important early Christian theologian whose writings about angels – how the Many related to the One – have been very controversial. For many centuries, Dionysius was thought to be the Areopagite whom Paul met in Athens (Acts 17.34), and his writings evidence for early Christian teaching. Modern scholars, however, place him in Syria in the late fifth century CE, hence the name Pseudo-Dionysius. His work is no longer seen as evidence for primitive Christianity but as a later fusion of Christianity and Platonism/ Neoplatonism. The writings have been hugely influential in both Eastern and Western forms of Christianity, but became controversial in the Reformation when people first began to doubt that Dionysius was the New Testament figure who left an accurate account of early Christian thought. In particular, some Protestant scholars were not sympathetic to his 'Platonism'. Luther became particularly hostile, especially towards Dionysius' ideas about the heavenly nature of priesthood. 'There is scarce a line of sound scholarship in him', he wrote, and his mystical theology was more Platonist than Christian. 'If I had my way, no believing mind would give the least attention to these books.'[1]

Dionysius certainly did adopt some of his scheme from Platonism, but the question is: how much? How much of what he says about the One and Many, God and the angels and priesthood, *could* have been early Christian? When Dionysius gave Isaiah as an example of someone purified by *seraphim* so as to be able to contemplate the highest beings around the throne,[2] he said he had learned this from an (unnamed) teacher. Since this is temple mysticism, was the teacher another Christian, or a Neoplatonist philosopher? We do not know,

---

[1] M. Luther, *The Babylonian Captivity of the Church*, 7.4.
[2] Dionysius, *The Celestial Hierarchy* 300BCD, in *Pseudo-Dionysius. The Complete Works*, tr. C. Luibheid, New York: Paulist Press, 1987.

but it is usually assumed that the teacher was not Christian, and that the angel hierarchy was imported into Christianity. Dionysius sets out nine ranks of angels, for example, which seem to derive from Neoplatonic ideas and differ from those implied by the Bible and temple texts. The archangels he describes are one of the lowest ranks whereas temple tradition has them as one of the highest, standing round the throne.

But much of Dionysius' so-called 'Platonism' could have been drawn from temple theology, because 'Platonism', via Pythagoras, had temple roots. In his *Celestial Hierarchy* we find:

> Listen carefully to things sacredly said and be inspired by them in an initiation into inspired things. Keep these holy truths a secret in your hidden mind. Guard their unity safe from the multiplicity of what is profane . . .

> A hierarchy is a sacred order, a state of understanding and an activity approximating as closely as possible to the divine . . .

> The goal of a hierarchy is to enable things to be as like as possible to God and to be at one with him.[3]

> Through [the angels'] mediating efforts, he who is the Cause and indeed the author of all purification has brought out from the domain of the hidden, the workings of his own providence down to the point where they are visible to us.[4]

This sounds very like temple mysticism, and so we now look at some ideas about the plurality and unity of the angels that *could* have been known to the early Christians in so far as they are found in contemporary or earlier Hebrew and Jewish texts, and so *could* have come to Dionysius from his Christian teachers.

The hosts of heaven

One of the great problems in the Hebrew scriptures is how to translate the word for God, *'elohim*. The word has a plural form, and yet translators usually choose 'God' singular and explain the plural as

---

[3] Dionysius, *Celestial Hierarchy*, 154C, 164D, 165A.
[4] Dionysius, *Celestial Hierarchy*, 308A.

a 'plural of majesty/divinity'. Judging from the context, the word sometimes appears to refer to God in the singular, and sometimes to 'gods' or 'heavenly beings' in the plural. The meaning can change from one to the other even in the same verse. The best example of the problem is Psalm 82.1: *''elohim* has taken his place in the assembly of *'el*; in the midst of *'elohim* he gives judgement.'[5] The verbs are singular, so the first *'elohim* must be 'God', but 'in the midst of *'elohim*' implies that there were several *'elohim*. It is left to the translator to make a decision: singular or plural. The usual rendering here is: 'God has taken his place in the divine council; in the midst of the gods he holds judgement.' But what of the *Shema*'? 'The LORD our *'elohim* is One.' Is this saying that the LORD is singular or plural? Or that the many are a unity?

And what should we do with other plural forms that seem to mean a singular but are not usually explained as a 'plural of majesty/divinity'? The enigmatic female figure Wisdom (e.g. Prov. 8.1) can also be 'Wisdoms' calling out to her children: 'I will pour out my Spirit on you' (Prov. 1.20, 23, translating literally, also 9.1). The Living One(s) in Ezekiel's vision of the chariot throne are sometimes singular, sometimes plural, and have the Spirit within the wheels (Ezek. 1.20; 10.17), yet neither Wisdom nor the Living One is usually thought of as divine. Much depends on the translator, and if he is already certain what a text means before he starts, he chooses his words accordingly. Thus the 'Living One', whom the temple mystics knew as the Lady of the temple,[6] is even translated 'the animal'.[7] There is always this problem where there are words with several meanings, and never more so than with the problem of singular and plural in the matter of God or 'gods', the hosts of heaven.

The simultaneous plurality and unity of the divine is never explained in biblical texts. Take the familiar story of the creation of Adam. *''elohim* said [sing.] "Let us make [pl.] Adam/human [sing.] in our image and as our likeness, and let them [pl.] have rule ..." So *'elohim* created [sing.] the Adam/human as his image, as the image of *'elohim* he created [sing.] him, male and female he created [sing.] them [pl.]' (Gen. 1.26–27). Is *'elohim* singular, as most of the verbs

---

[5] See above, p. 46.
[6] See below, p. 111.
[7] Ezekiel 1.20, JB.

imply, or plural? And if Adam is male and female, can the singular *'elohim* have a plural image that is male and female?

There are also texts which show that it was normal temple thinking to represent the LORD as one angel or several. Josephus, for example, paraphrased the story of Abraham meeting the LORD and two men, or was it three men, or were they all angels? Genesis itself is not clear (Gen. 18.1, 2, 16, 22; 19.1). When he retold the story, Josephus did not mention the LORD, which might seem a curious omission, unless it was natural for him, an educated Jew from the high priestly family, to think that an angel, or three angels, was another way of describing the LORD. Three angels, he wrote, came to Abraham at Mamre: one to tell him of the birth of Isaac and two to destroy Sodom.[8] The later Jewish reading of the story is the same: the LORD appeared to Abraham but he/they were indeed three angels. When Abraham spoke to one of them – 'my lord'[9] (Gen. 18.3) – he was addressing Michael, their leader, who came to tell him that Isaac would be born,[10] and the two who went on to Sodom were Gabriel, to destroy the city, and Raphael, to rescue Lot.[11] The early Christians said this had been a pre-incarnation appearance of Jesus, and Constantine had a great church built at Mamre to mark the place where 'the Son of God appeared to Abraham with two angels . . . He who, for the salvation of mankind, was born of a Virgin, there manifested himself to a godly man.'[12] Ikons of this scene are said to represent the Trinity, Jewish tradition says three archangels, and the original text is not clear.

Plurality and unity is assumed in texts that describe archangels. Sometimes they are seven, sometimes four or three, but always they are One. They look the same, they act together. In the sixth heaven, Enoch saw seven archangels, all looking the same, dressed in the same way, and acting together to uphold the harmony of creation.[13] Elsewhere, *1 Enoch* names seven archangels as the watching ones:[14] three of the seven took Enoch up onto a tower to see all history set before

---

[8] Josephus, *Antiquities* 1.11.
[9] Just the term of respect, not the Name.
[10] *Genesis Rabbah* XLVIII.1, 10.
[11] *Genesis Rabbah* L.1, 2.
[12] Sozomen, *History* 2.4.
[13] *2 Enoch* 19.1–4.
[14] *1 Enoch* 20.1–7.

him,[15] but four are named as the four presences/faces on the four sides of the LORD of Spirits, Enoch's equivalent to the LORD of Hosts.[16] Enoch does not mention the throne here, but the LORD is in the midst of thousands of angels, and so the scene is that of Revelation 4. The four presences/faces are Michael, Raphael, Gabriel and Phanuel,[17] the fourfold Presence, and yet no evidence survives for how the four related to the Angel of the Presence. There was debate in the second temple period over the status of the Angel of the Presence because the Greek translation of Isaiah 63.9 – 'the angel of his presence' – emphasized that this meant the LORD himself, 'not an ambassador nor an angel, but he himself' (Lxx Isa. 63.9). The LORD was present in/as the Angel. The blessing for the Zadokite priests at Qumran was: 'May you attend upon the service of the temple in the Kingdom, and decree destiny with the Angels of the Presence . . .'[18] The priests in the temple served and ruled with/as the manifold presence of the LORD himself.

The evidence for this unity/plurality in temple discourse is consistent over many centuries. The four presences/faces had earlier been the four throne names of the one king: 'His name will be called "Wonderful Counsellor, Mighty God, Everlasting Father, Prince of Peace" . . . upon the throne of David and over his kingdom . . .' (Isa. 9.6–7). Now in Hebrew 'Everlasting Father' is identical to 'Father of Booty', i.e. triumphant warrior,[19] a meaning which makes the four throne names correspond to the names of the four archangels:

- Wonderful Counsellor = Uriel, whose name means 'Light of God';
- Mighty God = Gabriel, whose name means 'Strength of God';
- Father of Booty = Michael, the warrior whose name means 'who is like God';
- Prince of Peace = Raphael, whose name means 'the healing of God'.

---

[15] *1 Enoch* 87.3; 90.31.

[16] *1 Enoch* 40.1–2.

[17] Phanuel is also called Uriel, *1 Enoch* 40.9, cf. *1 Enoch* 10.1. Phanuel means 'face of God', and Uriel means 'light of God', so the names have the same meaning. The LORD of Hosts has four 'faces', which in Greek would be *prosopa*, the word that became the 'persons' of the Trinity.

[18] *Blessings*, 1QSb IV.

[19] F. Brown, R. Driver, C. Briggs, *A Hebrew and English Lexicon of the Old Testament*, Oxford: Clarendon Press, 1962 edn, p. 723.

In the Greek, the four throne names became just one: Angel of Great Counsel/Design (Lxx Isa. 9.6). Now the one who ruled on the throne of David would, like Solomon, have sat on the throne of the LORD as king and been worshipped. In other words, the LORD could be described as 'the Angel of Great Counsel' or with the names of the four archangels who were his Presence(s).

John saw seven angels, all identical and wearing golden girdles. They were the sevenfold presence of the high priest because only the high priest wore a golden girdle (Rev. 15.5–6).[20] Since the high priest 'was' the presence of the LORD in the temple – he wore the Name on his forehead and was the one who came with/in the Name of the LORD – John saw the sevenfold presence as the seven archangels, each the high priest. John saw Jesus dressed in the same way (Rev. 1.13), but Jesus too thought of himself as plurally present in his followers: 'Where two or three are gathered in my name, there am I in the midst of them' (Matt. 18.20). Paul learned this on the road to Damascus, if he had not known it already. He was persecuting Jesus' followers, and heard the voice asking 'Why do you persecute me?' (Acts 9.4). Jesus was realizing in his followers one of the central beliefs of temple mysticism: 'The LORD our *'elohim*, the LORD is One.'

The now-incomplete treatise on astronomy in *1 Enoch* 72—82 reveals more about the angels and their unity. This astronomy book is a complicated set of calendrical calculations, the only extensive evidence for the ancient Jews' fame as astronomers. Theophrastus, a Greek writing about 300 BCE and the earliest Gentile to write about the Jews, said of them: 'They converse with each other about the deity and at night time make observations of the stars, gazing at them and calling on God in prayer.'[21] Uriel revealed all this knowledge to Enoch, and showed him how each quarter day (and quarter?) was ruled by one great angel, and then each month by other angels, and each day within the month by lesser angels.[22] This implies that the angels of the days were somehow 'under' the angels of the months, and they in turn 'under' the angels of the quarters. This was, however, not just

---

[20] Josephus, *Antiquities* 3.159.

[21] Theophrastus, *De Pietate*, quoted in M. Stern, *Greek and Latin Authors on Jews and Judaism*, Jerusalem: Israel Academy of Sciences and Humanities, 1974, vol. 1, p. 10.

[22] *1 Enoch* 82.10–14.

a simple hierarchy, because all the lesser angels were 'included' in the greater angels.

One of the texts found in a cave at Nag Hammadi in Egypt in 1945, and labelled 'gnostic', was the *Letter of Eugnostos*, which existed in two forms: the original 'letter' and an expanded version entitled *The Wisdom of Jesus Christ*. It was considered compatible with Christian teaching, even though it was itself pre-Christian, and the community who hid their library in the cave doubtless thought of themselves as Christian. Several of the Nag Hammadi texts are hostile to the religion of the Old Testament and its interpreters, but the authors still conducted their discourse in terms of its stories. They seem to have shared a heritage with the Jews, but had parted company over some fundamentals. The period immediately after the exile and the 'Ezra' influence are likely to have been factors in this parting of the ways, and the amount of temple imagery in the texts suggests they were written by people who disagreed with the Deuteronomists.

Many passages in the Nag Hammadi books are familiar, for example this from the *Tripartite Tractate*:

> Those who have listened to what [the prophets] said concerning [the vision and the unity] do not reject any of it, but have accepted the scriptures in an altered way. By interpreting them, they established many heresies which have existed to the present among the Jews. Some say that God is One, who made a proclamation in the ancient scriptures. Others say that he is many . . . Still others say that he is the creator of that which has come into being. Still others say that it was by his angels that he created . . . The prophets, however, did not say anything of their own accord but each of them [spoke] of the things which he had seen and heard through the proclamation of the Saviour.[23]

Vision, unity and plurality, and recognizing that the LORD who spoke through the prophets was the Saviour. This is not the way the Old Testament is usually read, but it would have been familiar to the early Church, and so the ('gnostic') observations about the nature of angels may have been available to the first Christians.

The original *Letter of Eugnostos* explains the unity and plurality of angels in terms of units of time, something that is compatible with

---

[23] *Tripartite Tractate*, Coptic Gnostic Library (hereafter CG) I.5.112–13.

the Enochic calendar revelations. Just as all the larger units of time contain within themselves the smaller units – the hours contain the minutes and the minutes the seconds – so the ranks of angels are all contained within each other and the One. In the language of these Gnostics, the various angels were the ranks of being that were in, and then came forth from, the holy of holies. In their code, the Immortal Man is Yahweh, the First Begetter is the heavenly Adam made as the divine son (cf. Luke 3.38). The third figure is uncertain because there is a break in the text, but other parts of the *Letter* show that he was the Saviour, the Second Adam.

- 'Our aeon came to be as a type in relation to Immortal Man.' (*Yahweh*)
- 'Time came to be as a type of the First Begetter, his son.' (*Adam*)
- '[The year] came to be as a type of the [****? the Saviour].' (*Second Adam Jesus*)
- 'The twelve months came to be as as a type of the twelve powers.' (*the disciples*)
- 'In relation to the angels who came from these, who are without number, the hours and moments of the days came to be as a type.' (*the Christians*)[24]

Just as time contains all its smaller units, so too Yahweh 'contains' his Son Adam and the Second Adam, the 12 apostles, and the numerous other Christians who were joined to them. Wherever this came from could have been the source of Dionysius' angel hierarchy too. The words that John attributed to Jesus are more familiar and say the same thing about the unity of the angels.

> I do not pray for these [the disciples] only, but also for those who believe in me through their word, that they may all be one; even as thou, Father, art in me, and I in thee, that they also may be in us, so that the world may believe that thou hast sent me.
>
> (John 17.20–21)

There are other familiar passages from these gnostic texts: 'The Saviour was a bodily image of the Unitary One. He is the totality in bodily form.'[25] Apparently enigmatic, this saying is perfectly comprehensible

---

[24] *Letter of Eugnostos*, CG III.3.84.
[25] *Tripartite Tractate*, CG I.5.116.

within the context of the *Shema'* and of temple mysticism. The Saviour was the One in human form, and the One was the totality of the heavenly beings. Paul's letter to Colossae said this too: 'For in him all the fullness, *plerōma*, of God was pleased to dwell' (Col. 1.19); and 'For in him the whole fullness, *plerōma*, of deity dwells bodily' (Col. 2.9). Clement of Alexandria preserved as quotations the teachings of Theodotus, a Gnostic. This is how he explained the role of Jesus uniting all Christians:

> They say that our angels were put forth as a unity and are one in that they came out from One. Now since we were in a divided state, Jesus was baptized so that the undivided should be divided until he should unite us with them in the fullness [*plerōma*], so we, the many, having become one, should all be mingled in the One which was divided for our sakes.[26]

There is a similar saying of Jesus in the *Gospel of Thomas*, which was found at Nag Hammadi in 1945: 'I am he who exists from the undivided . . . Therefore I say, If he is [undivided] he will be filled with light, but if he is divided he will be filled with darkness.'[27] This is the context for the familiar lines in Ephesians, where there is so much language from temple mysticism – unity, knowledge, fullness, that is, the undivided: 'that you may be filled with all the fullness, *plerōma*, of God' (Eph. 3.19); 'until we all attain to the unity of the faith and of the knowledge of the Son of God, to mature manhood, to the measure of the stature of the fullness, *plerōma*, of Christ . . .' (Eph. 4.13).

Unity and plurality, the unity of the LORD and the *'elohim*, were central to the temple mysteries, and from the beginning, Christian teachers said that the Church on earth was like angels, both in respect of worship and of unity. Clement, bishop of Rome at the end of the first century CE, wrote this to the quarrelling Christians of Corinth: 'Think of the vast company of angels who all wait on him to serve his wishes . . . In the same way we ought ourselves in *a conscious unity*, to cry to him as it were with one voice, if we are to obtain a share of his glorious great promises.'[28]

---

[26] *Excerpts from Theodotus* 36.
[27] *Gospel of Thomas* 61.
[28] *1 Clement* 34, my emphasis.

Fire and light

The unity and plurality were often expressed with the images of fire and light, and these too are found in texts over many centuries. We shall look at examples from the first temple, from the second temple period, and from the early Church: from Ezekiel, a priest in the sixth century BCE, from the Qumran *Songs of the Sabbath Sacrifice* used, we assume, by a priestly community in the time of Jesus, and from Justin, a Christian writer born in Palestine and teaching in Rome in the mid-second century CE. Christian imagery is deeply rooted in temple mysticism.

When Justin was debating Christian belief with a Jew, he explained that God 'begetting' did not mean cutting off something new from its source but rather extending the source. The One begotten in the beginning, he said, 'was begotten of the Father by an act of will . . . yet not by cutting off . . . just as we see also happening in the case of a fire, which is not lessened when it has kindled another, but remains the same, and that which has been kindled by it likewise appears to exist by itself, not diminishing that from which it was kindled'.[29] Later he used the light of the sun as an illustration of the same point:

> The Power sent from the Father of all [the Son] is indivisible and inseparable from the Father, just as they say the light of the sun is indivisible and inseparable from the sun in the heavens. The Father, when he chooses, causes his power to spring forth, and when he chooses he makes it return to himself. In this way . . . he made the angels.[30]

The fiery unity and plurality of the angels, often called the sons of God, and the four faces/presences of the LORD were images later modified to describe (but not explain) the Trinity, whose 'persons', *prosōpa*, are the Greek equivalent of the Hebrew face/presence, *pānim*, a plural form (*another* plural form!). The familiar words of the Nicene Creed come from temple mysticism and its angels. The Son of God was 'eternally begotten of the Father' – meaning he was begotten in eternity, in the holy of holies[31] – 'God from God, Light from Light, true God from true God, begotten not made . . .'

---

[29] Justin, *Dialogue with Trypho* 61.
[30] Justin, *Trypho* 128.
[31] We shall return to this. See below, pp. 101–2.

The holy of holies in Solomon's temple was a cube-shaped oracle lined with gold, and it represented the pre-created light and a cube of fire. The earliest descriptions of the functioning holy of holies are the visions of Ezekiel, when he described the chariot throne alive with fiery beings. The first characteristic of both these accounts (the throne arriving in Babylon in chapter 1 and the throne leaving the temple in chapter 10) is the mixture of singular and plural forms of both nouns and verbs, and the fluidity of gender. The texts are impossible to translate both accurately and coherently. We shall return to this,[32] but at the moment we are concerned with the images of fire. The throne was flashing fire within a fiery cloud, and from the fire came the 'likeness' of four living creatures (Ezek. 1.4–5). The most literal translation is the AV, which best conveys the sense of bewilderment and confusion:

> As for the likeness of the living creatures, their appearance was like burning coals of fire, and like the appearance of lamps: it went up and down among the living creatures; and the fire was bright, and out of the fire went forth lightning. And the living creatures ran and returned as the appearance of a flash of lightning. (Ezek. 1.13–14)

Over this fire was a throne, with a human figure upon it, and he too was fiery. 'This was the appearance of the likeness of the glory of the LORD' (Ezek. 1.28, AV). The glory of the LORD in the cloud had left the temple (Ezek. 10.4), but before it departed a man clothed in linen had entered the chariot throne itself: 'Go in among the whirling wheels underneath the cherubim; fill your hands with burning coals from between the cherubim, and scatter them over the city' (Ezek. 10.2). This is the earliest evidence for a human figure – here already transformed into an angel, 'a man in linen' – entering the domain of the heavenly throne. And this is also the earliest evidence for the plurality of the throne described as lamps/torches of fire. Elsewhere Ezekiel imagined Eden as a mountain-top garden of *'elohim*, gods, where an anointed guardian *cherub* walked in the midst of stones, *'abney*, of fire. Remove one consonant and they become sons, *b*e*ney*, of fire (Ezek. 28.14). On his heavenly journey, Enoch saw such beings; they were like flaming fire and could take human form: 'They [the angel guides] took me to a place in which

---

[32] See below, pp. 110–11.

those who were there were like flaming fire, and when they wished, they appeared as men.'[33] In another vision he described sons of God clad in white, walking on flames of fire, and countless angels encircling the holy of holies.[34]

The Qumran *Songs of the Sabbath Sacrifice* give the best glimpse of the holy of holies as people imagined it in the time of Jesus. As in Ezekiel's vision, the fire around the chariot throne was alive, but the *Songs* name the living fire as the *'elohim*, or the *'ēlim*, both meaning gods:

> From between his glorious wheels, there is as it were a fiery vision of most holy spirits. About them the appearance of rivulets of fire in the likeness of gleaming brass . . . many-coloured glory, marvellous pigments, clearly mingled, spirits of the living *'elohim* moving to and fro . . .[35]

> At their marvellous stations are spirits, many-coloured like the work of a weaver, splendid engraved figures. In the midst of a glorious appearance of scarlet, colours of the most holy spiritual light . . . These are . . . the princes of the kingdom, the kingdom of the holy ones of the king of holiness . . .[36]

The fiery spirits of the *Sabbath Songs* served as priests in the heavenly temple, but nobody knows if these songs are an imaginary picture of heaven, or a description of the actual temple service in Jerusalem, where the priests 'were' the angels, as the prophet Malachi had reminded them (Mal. 2.7, my translation: 'a priest . . . is the angel of the LORD of Hosts'). The spirits were described as the gods of knowledge and righteousness: 'all the gods, *'ēlim*, of knowledge celebrate his glory, and all the spirits of righteousness celebrate his truth', 'the gods, *'ēlim*, of knowledge enter by the doors of glory . . .'[37]

Those who entered the light were transformed by it and reflected the light into the world. This was the role of an angel of the presence. The Qumran priests were blessed, as we have seen, with the words 'May you be as an angel of the Presence . . .' but the blessing then

[33] *1 Enoch* 17.1.

[34] *1 Enoch* 71.1, 8.

[35] *Songs of the Sabbath Sacrifice*, 4Q405.20.

[36] *Songs of the Sabbath Sacrifice*, 4Q405.23.

[37] *Songs of the Sabbath Sacrifice*, 4Q403.1, 4Q405.23.

reveals what an angel of the Presence has to do: 'May He make you holy among his people, and an [eternal] light [to illumine] the world with knowledge and to enlighten the face of the congregation [with wisdom].'[38] The role of the angels was to bring light and knowledge. An Enoch text which the Qumran community possessed said this knowledge would be restored at the end of the 'seventh week', that is, at the end of the second temple period: '[Then] the chosen ones will be given sevenfold wisdom and knowledge.'[39] The chosen ones would be in the light of eternal life.[40] Philo also described this light, and how it lost some of its brilliance as it came into the material creation:

> The invisible light, perceptible only by the mind, which was created as an image of the divine Logos, who made its creation known . . . It could be called the all-brightness[41] . . . for the unmixed and pure radiance begins to dim when it starts the inevitable change from the world of the mind to the visible world . . .[42]

Paul wrote to the Christians of Corinth that they were reflecting the glory of the LORD: 'We all, with unveiled faces[43] reflecting the glory of the LORD, are being changed into his likeness from one degree of glory to another . . .' (2 Cor. 3.18, my translation). Thus too Peter, who wrote of the Christians as the priestly people of the light who 'declare the wonderful deeds', i.e. teach: 'You are a chosen race, a royal priesthood, a holy nation, God's own people, that you may declare the wonderful deeds of him who called you out of darkness into his marvellous light' (1 Pet. 2.9). And this is why, in traditional Christian art, both angels and saints have haloes; they reflect the glory they have seen and, like Moses, have been bathed in the invisible light.

The Qumran priests knew they stood in the light: 'I shall shine forth with sevenfold light[ ] you have established me (for) your glory.'[44]

---

[38] *The Blessings*, 1QSb IV.

[39] *1 Enoch* 93.10; 4QEn^g.

[40] *1 Enoch* 58.3.

[41] The equivalent of sevenfold.

[42] Philo, *Creation* 31.

[43] A reference to Moses who had to veil his face after he had been with the LORD, lest his transfigured state should dazzle the people of Israel; Exod. 34.29–35.

[44] *Hymns*, 1QH XV.27.

'And stand [ ] in the everlasting abode, illumined with perfect light for ever.'[45] They sang their thanksgiving:

> You shine out to me in your strength . . .
> By me you have illumined the faces of many
> And you are strong beyond telling
> You have taught me your wonderful mysteries and
>   your wonderful counsel,
> And you have been my strength.[46]
>
> By your insight/understanding [? you have given
>   me knowledge]
> And by your glory my light shines forth
> Light from darkness . . .[47]

John described the enthroned Lamb in the same way, but he used the temple code of seven eyes and seven horns. Sevenfold meant complete, and so the seven eyes meant that the Lamb had received the sevenfold Spirit and was the totality of the seven archangels. In other words, he was the LORD. In the sixth century BCE, Zechariah learned from an angel that the lamps of the seven-branched candlestick represented the seven 'eyes' of the LORD on earth (Zech. 4.2, 10), and John had seen these seven spirits as fiery torches before the throne (Rev. 4.5). The Lamb's seven horns were seven beams of light,[48] the sevenfold light that the *Hymn* mentioned, but the 'horns' show that this vision was originally 'thought' in Hebrew. The Hebrew verb 'send out beams of light', is written in the same way as 'horn'.[49]

This curious confusion is best illustrated by the account of Moses' face shining with rays of light when he came down from Sinai (Exod. 34.29, 30, 35). He is often depicted coming from Sinai with two horns, because Jerome translated the word into Latin as 'horned', *cornuta*: '[Moses] did not know that his face had grown horns through talking with the LORD.'[50] A text from the time of Jesus, formerly attributed

---

[45] 1QH XXI.27–8.

[46] 1QH XII.24b, 28, 29.

[47] 1QH XVII.26.

[48] Hebrew 'horn'.

[49] Shine is *qāran*, horn is *qeren*, but the written consonants are identical.

[50] Vulgate, Exodus 34.29: *Ignorabat quod cornuta esse facies sua ex consortio sermonis Domini.*

to Philo, shows how this shining face was actually understood at that time. Note that the top of Sinai is assumed to be the holy of holies, because it was the presence of the LORD.

> Moses came down [from Sinai]. And when he had been bathed with the invisible light, he went down to the place where the light of the sun and moon are: and the light of his face surpassed the splendour of the sun and the moon, and he did not even know this . . .[51]

When Moses was about to die and had learned the plan of history from the LORD, 'He was filled with understanding and his appearance became glorious.'[52] Then the LORD appointed Joshua as his successor: 'Take [Moses'] garments of wisdom and clothe yourself, and with his belt of knowledge gird your loins, and you will be changed and become another man.'[53] The garments of the illuminated ones were garments of wisdom, and the ones who wore them were transformed.[54]

The *Wisdom of Jesus Christ* is one of the texts found at Nag Hammadi, and although it is damaged, enough can be read to see that it describes the heavenly Adam, his place of light called the kingdom, and the angels who reflect the divine light. There are no shadows because the whole place is light; there is not one single source. This may be why there are no shadows in ikons; they depict the same reality.

> First-Begetter father is called Adam, [ ] eye of the light, because he came from the shining light [ ] his holy angels who are ineffable (and) shadowless. They rejoice continually with joy in their reflecting, which they received from their Father, (this is) the whole Kingdom of the Son of Man, the one who is called Son of God. (It) is full of ineffable and shadowless joy, and unchanging jubilation because they rejoice over his imperishable glory . . .
>
> I came from the Self begotten and the First Endless Light so that I might reveal everything to you.[55]

The Qumran community thought of themselves as people born from the light, the children of light, and their *Community Rule* included this instruction for their leader:

[51] Pseudo-Philo, *Biblical Antiquities*, 12.1.
[52] Pseudo-Philo, *Biblical Antiquities*, 19.16.
[53] Pseudo-Philo, *Biblical Antiquities*, 20.2.
[54] See below, p. 137.
[55] *Wisdom of Jesus Christ*, CG III.4.105–6.

The Master shall instruct all the children of light . . .

All the children of righteousness are ruled by the Prince of Light and walk in the ways of light . . .

The God of Israel and his Angel of truth will succour all the sons of light.[56]

They saw themselves as warriors, literally, against the forces of darkness, which were at that time manifested in the Romans and their allies. Their battle hymn reveals the cosmic context of their illumination. The chosen ones were instructed in the laws, learned in wisdom; they had heard the voice of majesty and had seen the holy angels; and their ears had been unstopped to hear profound things. There follows a paean to the Creator, and then: 'Truly the battle is thine!' The Prince of Light and his angels would fight with them on earth, and they were confident of victory. 'With everlasting light he will enlighten with joy [the children] of Israel; peace and blessing shall be with the company of God.'[57] These images are found in Revelation too: the Lamb with his thousands massed on Mount Zion and then the armies of heaven riding out on white horses (Rev. 14.1; 19.11–16).

In the New Testament, it was John who most used the imagery of light and its children, although it was not unique to him. Luke attributed 'light' imagery to Jesus – his followers as sons of light (Luke 16.8) – and Paul warned the Christians in Corinth that Satan could disguise himself as an angel of light (2 Cor. 11.14). John knew that with Jesus the Light of Day One had come into the world, and that everything which had formerly been the privilege of the temple mystics who entered the holy of holies – whether literally as high priests or in their visions – was possible for his followers. 'He who has seen me has seen the Father' (John 14.9). They would become sons of God, they would be part of the unity, and they would have the heavenly knowledge.

The true light that enlightens every man was coming into the world. He was in the world, and the world was made through him . . . To all who received him, who believed in his name, he gave power to become children of God . . . We have beheld his glory . . .

(John 1.9, 10, 12, 14)

---

[56] *Community Rule*, 1QS III.
[57] *War Scroll*, 1QM X, XIII, XVII.

I am the light of the world; he who follows me will not walk in darkness, but will have the light of life.   (John 8.12)

While you have the light, believe in the light, that you may become sons of light.   (John 12.36)

The practical application of this is presented in John's first letter. The children of light have been anointed by the Holy One and have received knowledge (1 John 2.20). Christians walk in the light as God is in the light (1 John 1.7), and John emphasized that the light and life also entailed love, the practical working out of unity. 'He who says he is in the light and hates his brother is in the darkness still' (1 John 2.9); 'We know that we have passed out of death into life, because we love the brethren' (1 John 3.14).

The *Gospel of Thomas* kept much of the temple setting of the sons of light and is best understood in that context.

> The disciples said to Jesus, 'Tell us how our end will be?' Jesus said, 'Have you discovered, then, the beginning that you look for the end? For where the beginning is, there the end will be. Blessed is he who will take his place in the beginning. He will know the end and will not experience death.'[58]

The disciples, having taken their place in the holy of holies, the beginning, and become sons of light, know their destiny and have passed beyond death into Life, cf. 'We know that we have passed out of death into life, because we love the brethren' (1 John 3.14). Elsewhere Thomas's Jesus used different imagery for the same teaching:

> Blessed are the *solitary* and the elect, for you will find the kingdom. For you are from it and to it you will return.
>   If they say to you, 'Where did you come from?' say to them, 'We came from the light, the place where the light came into being on its own accord, and established itself and became manifest through their image.'[59]

Since the *Gospel of Thomas* is a collection of sayings, their order may not be significant, but these two do make sense as a pair. The kingdom was the holy of holies, the place of light, as we have seen,[60] and so

---

[58] *Gospel of Thomas* 18.
[59] *Gospel of Thomas* 49, 50.
[60] See above, pp. 44–5.

the sayings are in effect duplicates. The 'they' who question the children of light may be the cherubim who were set to guard the way to the tree of life (Gen. 3.24), to which Jesus had promised access for his faithful followers (Rev. 2.7; 22.14).

The 'elect' needs no explanation, but nobody knows for certain who was meant by the solitary, *monachos*. Perhaps it meant a monk or celibate – as it did later – but another saying suggests that in the earliest period it meant those who were entitled to enter the holy of holies. 'Jesus said, "Many are standing at the door, but it is the solitary who will enter the bridal chamber."'[61] The bridal chamber, as we shall see,[62] was yet another name for the holy of holies, the place where the sons of God were born, and so 'solitary' may not be the best way to translate a word derived from 'one'. It may imply someone who was already part of the Unity, someone who had been restored to the undivided state of the original Adam, before the Adam was divided into male and female in the material creation. The child newly born in the holy of holies would have become wise, like Adam before he/they chose the wrong tree. The newborn would have entered the place of light, the kingdom, and thus be able to teach those who were old in the ways of the world.

> Jesus said, 'The man old in days will not hesitate to ask a small child seven days old about the place of life, and he will live. For many who are first will become last, and they will become "solitary" and the same.'[63]

Children entering the kingdom may have been the original context for Jesus' saying: 'whoever does not receive the kingdom of God like a child shall not enter it' (Mark 10.15). In fact, there may be several of Jesus' sayings whose original context was temple mysticism, but whose deeper meaning was lost when temple tradition ceased to be the context in which his teachings were understood.

The *Gospel of Thomas* also has a saying reminiscent of one of the Qumran *Hymns*, about someone whose light illuminated the congregation: 'Jesus said, "There is light within a man of light, and he/it

---

[61] *Gospel of Thomas* 75. 'Solitary' is also found in *Gospel of Thomas* 11, 16, 22, 23 and 106.
[62] See below, p. 105.
[63] *Gospel of Thomas* 4.

lights up the whole world." [64] And the light and unity that extended to include Jesus' disciples is recalled in: 'Jesus said, "I am the light which is above them all. It is I who am the All. From me did the All come forth and unto me did the all extend." [65] Paul used these ideas to explain Christian unity, that all Christians have returned from the state of plurality into the unity of Christ: 'There is neither Jew nor Greek, there is neither slave nor free, there is neither male nor female; for you are all one in Christ Jesus' (Gal. 3.28).

Heavenly music

From the time of the first temple, the unity of the many was not only described in visual terms – fire, light – but also as music. The heavenly beings sang the praises of the Creator (Ps. 148.1–2), and this was replicated on earth in the music of the temple 'with one voice' (2 Chron. 5.13, my translation). The best known angels in the New Testament were heard by the Bethlehem shepherds, praising God and proclaiming peace (i.e. *shalōm*, wholeness, oneness) on earth (Luke 2.13–14). The earliest Christian picture of heaven has countless angels and heavenly beings singing a 'new song' to the Lamb on the throne (Rev. 5.9), and 'new', as we shall see, implied renewal and healing.

Temple mystics imagined the creation held together by the bonds of the everlasting covenant or woven as a fabric. When the bonds were broken by sin, the whole creation collapsed and had to be renewed and healed. Music both enabled and represented this healing, ritualized in the temple as atonement. John's vision of the music of heaven shows the healing (Rev. 4.8–11), and Isaiah left a vivid picture of the creation collapsing:

> The earth mourns and withers,
> The world languishes and withers;
> The heavens languish together with the earth.
> The earth lies polluted under its inhabitants;
> For they have transgressed the laws,
> Violated the statutes,
> Broken the everlasting covenant.   (Isa. 24.4–5)

---

[64] *Gospel of Thomas* 24.
[65] *Gospel of Thomas* 77.

The broken covenant bonds were repaired by atonement, especially the ritual of the day of atonement. This was part of the old new-year festival in the autumn, which celebrated and re-enacted the original creation and then restored the broken covenant bonds. The climax was the feast of Tabernacles, which celebrated the enthronement of the King over the renewed creation. In Revelation, John described the King (the Lamb) being enthroned after the great day of atonement on Good Friday.

The Jewish heirs of the temple mystics were the *merkavah* mystics, who often spoke of the bonds and the fabric of creation. Although the 'fabric' may have been their own interpretation of the veil where they saw all history, the bonds of the eternal covenant were known in the time of the first temple. They bound into one system heaven and earth, human society and the wider creation. The bonds and the bounds held the order of the cosmos secure. Job knew that the stars were bound in their courses (Job 38.31); Jeremiah knew that the LORD had set bounds for the sea (Jer. 5.22); the psalmist knew that the earth and its seasons had their bounds (Ps. 74.17), as did the rulers of the earth who tried to break free (Ps. 2.3). Proverbs 8 gives a glimpse of creation described in this way: the Creator drew a circle on the deep, assigned the sea its limit and marked out the foundations of the earth (Prov. 8.27–29).[66] R. Nehunyah, who lived in Emmaus at the end of the first century CE, ascended to the throne and saw 'the mysteries and the secrets, the bonds and wonders . . . the weaving of the web that completes the world'.[67] Other mystics described these bonds as the mysteries.

Proverbs 8 shows that this system of bonds and bounds was imagined as music. The mysterious female figure 'Wisdom', who was beside the Creator as he established the creation, was the *'amōn*, a word otherwise unknown in the Hebrew scriptures. It was translated into Greek as *harmozousa*, 'the woman who holds all things together in harmony'. Enoch had a different way to describe cosmic harmony. When he ascended to the sixth heaven, he saw there that group of seven identical archangels with glorious, shining faces, who were maintaining the unity of creation by music:

---

[66] There are many examples. We shall return to this in Chapter 4.
[67] *Hekhalot Rabbati* 201, using the numbering in P. Schäfer, *Synopse zur Hekhalot Literatur*, Tübingen: Mohr, 1981.

They put the commandments and instructions in order and the sweet choral singing and every kind of glorious praise. These are the archangels who are over the angels; and they harmonize all existence, heavenly and earthly; and angels who are over seasons and years, and angels who are over rivers and ocean, and angels who are over the fruits of the earth and over every kind of grass, and who give every kind of food to every kind of living thing . . .[68]

The great angels literally held the creation in harmony.

In the *Apocalypse of Abraham*, a late-second temple text, the (seven-fold) angel in charge of the other angels/powers of creation appeared to the patriarch as Yahweh-el, a single angel dressed as a high priest whose role was to keep order among the heavenly beings and to teach them the song. Presumably it was the song that maintained the good order. This was the angel(s) that Enoch saw, and Abraham addressed him as 'Singer of the Eternal One'.[69] The vision was accompanied by music. Abraham had to learn the heavenly song before he could approach the throne, and his angel guide told him: 'Worship, Abraham, and recite the song that I taught you.' Abraham sang, calling out the many names of God, and then: 'Renewing/restoring the age of the just, you make your light shine before the inner light upon your creation . . . in your heavenly dwelling place is an inexhaustible light of an inexpressible dawn, from the light of your face.'[70] The gist is clear even if the text is not.

Now this text is an expansion of Genesis 15, where the LORD appeared to Abram in a vision. The *Apocalypse of Abraham* shows the same phenomenon as does Josephus' account of the theophany at Mamre: where 'the LORD' appears in the Hebrew scriptures, the later writer could substitute an angel or several angels.[71] Here in this *Apocalypse*, the LORD – whose name means 'He who causes to be'[72] – was called *the Singer of creation*. Recalling that 'the LORD our *'elohim* is One', the unity of the LORD was expressed by the angel music, where each angel played a part in the one song. Thus singing 'with one voice' was an important element in temple and, later, in church music. How

[68] *2 Enoch* 19.1–4.
[69] *Apocalypse of Abraham* 10—12.
[70] *Apocalypse of Abraham* 17.5, 18—19.
[71] See above, p. 66.
[72] See below, pp. 122–3.

the temple songs were sung or the instruments played is not known, largely through problems of translation, but the musicians – players and singers – made music 'with one voice' (2 Chron. 5.13, my translation), imitating the angels. Although *harmozousa*, holding all things together in harmony, was used to describe the role of Wisdom in the creation, harmony in the modern sense was not known in temple music.[73] In the *Ascension of Isaiah*, 'Isaiah' saw the angels 'and they all sang praises with one voice'.[74] The Christians too: 'As the heavenly natures of the incorporeal powers do all glorify God with one consent, so also on earth all men with one mouth and with one purpose may glorify the only, the one and true God by Christ his only-begotten'.[75] 'The angelic choirs sing praise to God with psalms . . . celebrating with a common voice from many mouths.'[76] Singing with one voice represented the unity of the Christian community and also their union with/as the angels and the harmony of creation.

When David was establishing the worship of the LORD in Jerusalem, even before the temple itself was built, he appointed Levites to serve before the ark, and therefore before the throne, to invoke, to thank and to praise the LORD. Their music caused the glory to appear in the temple; it joined heaven and earth. Later writers made clear that the music on earth prompted the heavenly music to respond, but the idea may be very old indeed. Thus R. Ishmael, who taught in the early second century CE, described his ascent to stand before the throne: 'He enlightened my eyes and my heart to utter [praises]. And when I opened my mouth and sang praises before the throne of glory, the holy creatures below the throne of glory and above the throne repeated after me, saying "Holy Holy Holy", and "Blessed be the glory of the LORD in his dwelling place."'[77] The Christians kept this pattern: in the Liturgy of St John Chrysostom, late fourth century CE, the Sanctus begins with the choir (on earth) and is taken up by the clergy in the sanctuary (in heaven). The heavens answering

---

[73] It is possible that the psalm heading 'according to the *sheminith*' means 'octave', e.g. Ps. 6.1; and 'according to *'alamoth*' means 'women's voices', e.g. Ps. 46.1. See *The Jewish Encyclopedia*, New York: Funk and Wagnalls, 1901–6, 'Music'.

[74] *Ascension of Isaiah* 7.15; 9.18. This is a Jewish text expanded by Christians about 100 CE.

[75] *Apostolic Constitutions* 2.56.

[76] Gregory Nazianzus, *Carmina* 2.1.1.180. In Migne, *Patrologia Greco-Latina* XXXVII.991; I do not know of an English version.

[77] *3 Enoch* 1.12.

the earth, however, may be the meaning of an otherwise inexplicable passage in Hosea, from the eighth century BCE: 'In that day, says the LORD, I will make[78] the heavens respond, and they shall respond to the earth, and the earth shall respond with the grain, the wine and the oil . . .' (Hos. 2.21–22, my translation). When the heavens and the earth were in harmony, the earth was fertile, but, as Isaiah wrote, when the bonds were broken, heaven and earth withered.

The bonds of creation expressed in music explains the difficult lines of Psalm 19:

> The heavens are telling the glory of God;
> And the firmament proclaims his handiwork.
> Day to day pours forth speech,
> And night to night declares knowledge.
> There is no speech, nor are there words;
> Their voice is not heard;
> Yet their music[79] goes out through all the earth,
> And their words to the end of the world.
>
> (Ps. 19.1–4, my translation)

The silent music of the creation would then be similar to the invisible light of Day One – something beyond human experience that had to be expressed in human terms. The Hebrew scriptures often mention 'the heavens' praising the Creator, which meant the song of the angels acknowledging their obedience to the Creator. The Targums, which gave the sense of the Hebrew as ordinary people understood it, have more singing angels than is apparent from a literal reading of the Hebrew scriptures. The Targum, for example, translated 'Let the heavens rejoice' (1 Chron. 16.31) as 'Let the angels on high rejoice'; 'Let heaven and earth praise him' (Ps. 69.34) became 'Let *the angels of heaven* praise him . . .'; 'Let the heavens praise thy wonders' (Ps. 89.5) became in some versions 'Let *the angels in heaven* praise thy wonders . . .'; 'the heavens proclaim his righteousness . . .' (Ps. 97.6) became '*the angels of heaven* proclaim . . .'

The singing angels may be another link to Pythagoras, who taught about harmony and the music of the spheres. This was later

---

[78] Reading the verb as *hiph'il*.

[79] Brown, Driver, Briggs, *Hebrew and English Lexicon*, p. 876 suggests 'chord' as the meaning; the word is literally a line.

understood to mean the sound of the heavenly bodies moving and was criticized by Aristotle: 'The theory that the movement of the stars produces a harmony ... is nevertheless untrue.'[80] Music was, however, associated with the original acts of creation in the older creation story known to Job, and Pythagoras could have learned about this when he was a young man in 'Syria'. The music of creation is not mentioned in Genesis and neither are the angels, but the LORD asked Job: 'Where were you when I laid the foundation of the earth ... Who determined its measurements[81] ... *when the morning stars sang together, and all the sons of God shouted for joy?'* (Job 38.4, 5, 7). Angels making music accompanied the creation. One of the Qumran psalms is a hymn about the Creator: 'He divides light from obscurity, he establishes the dawn by the knowledge of his heart. When all his angels saw it, they sang, *rānan*, for he showed them that which they had not known.'[82] On the old new year's day[83] there was a solemn 'memory of the shout of joy' (Lev. 23.24, translating literally), most likely a memory of the creation since this was celebrated at the old new year; and the people *shouted for joy* when the foundations of the second temple were laid (Ezra 3.11, 12, 13). They were re-enacting the beginning of creation since the temple represented the creation. The Jubilee was the great restoration of the creation and of human society, and it too was proclaimed on the day of atonement with this same 'shout for joy' (Lev. 25.9, my translation).

In Job's creation story, the angels 'sang' *rānan*, which meant to make a ringing cry, not necessarily with a human voice, and the sons of God 'shouted for joy', *rua'*, which meant to shout or to make a blast on a horn or trumpet. It is interesting to see where these words occur elsewhere, translating literally: 'Let the nations be glad and *sing*' (Ps. 67.5), where the context is the LORD's face shining forth; '*they sing* about the majesty of the LORD' (Isa. 24.14) as the Righteous One appears for judgement and restoration; the desert will *sing* and the tongue of the dumb will *sing* as the people return to their land

---

[80] Aristotle, *On the Heavens* B9 290b12.

[81] Measurements, *middoth*, is the word later used to describe what the mystics learned before the throne, and then it is translated 'mysteries'.

[82] Non-biblical Psalms, 11Q5 XXVI.

[83] After the calendar change it became the first of the seventh month.

(Isa. 35.2, 6). 'Sing a new song ... *with shouts of joy*' (Ps. 33.3) as the
LORD establishes the creation; 'God has gone up *with a shout of joy*'
(Ps. 47.5) as the LORD ascends to his throne in triumph; 'Blessed are
the people who know the *shout of joy*, who walk, O LORD, in the light
of thy countenance ...' (Ps. 89.15). These are all new year themes:
judgement, renewal of the creation, and the LORD, the King, ascending
his throne and shining forth.

The temple represented the creation, and the temple service of
atonement renewed the creation. Simon the high priest taught that
the world was sustained by three things: by the Law, by the temple
service, and by loving kindness,[84] and Ben Sira has left a picture
of him serving in the temple on the day of atonement, 'until the
order of the LORD's *worship* was completed ...' (Ben Sira 50.19,
my translation).[85] The Greek word 'worship' here is *kosmos*, used in
Genesis 2.1 to describe the *order of creation* that had been completed.
The temple service on the day of atonement, with its singing, completed the LORD's order of creation. Even after the temple had been
destroyed, the role of the music was remembered. Interpreting 'I have
given the Levites as a gift to Aaron and his sons ... to make atonement ...' (Num. 8.19), R. Benaiah in the early third century CE said
the Levites made atonement with their singing in the temple.[86]

This was the context, too, for the 'new song'. There are many examples of the 'new' song in the Hebrew scriptures, and their contexts
suggest that the 'new' song might be better translated 'renewing' song,
associating the music with renewing the creation.[87] Psalm 33 exhorts
the musicians to a new song, and then describes how the LORD made
heaven and earth and rules the nations. In Psalm 96 the new song
is sung (according to the Targum, by the angels on high) because the
earth is established, the LORD reigns and is about to come as judge.
Psalm 98 is similar. Psalm 144 describes the new song for the LORD
who brings prosperity and victory, and Psalm 149 is similar. Isaiah
exhorted a new song as the LORD recreated his people (Isa. 42.10–25).
Given these contexts, it is significant that the 'new song' in John's

---

[84] Mishnah *Aboth* 1.2.
[85] He had just come out from the 'house of the veil', that is, the holy of holies, and the
high priest went there only on the day of atonement, Ben Sira 50.5.
[86] Jerusalem Talmud *Ta'anit* 4.2.
[87] The Hebrew root *ḥdš* from which our 'new' derives means to renew or repair.

vision was sung immediately the Lamb had been enthroned, and that the earth then joined in the liturgy (Rev. 5.9–14).

Temple mysticism was characterized by a mixing of the senses, since the whole experience was beyond normal words and sense perception. Enoch saw two men (that is, angels) whose faces shone like the sun. Their eyes were like lamps and fire came from their mouths, '*Their clothing was various singing*, and their arms were like wings of gold.'[88] When 'Isaiah' was in the seventh heaven, he both heard and saw the praise that was being sent up from the lower heavens.[89] Wordplay from the original Isaiah implies that the glory was heard as well as seen.[90] The mystics knew invisible light and inaudible music, both of which were the glory. This explains the otherwise curious choice of words in the Greek of Exodus 24: 'They saw the God of Israel; and there was under his feet as it were a pavement of sapphire stone . . . they beheld God, and ate and drank' (Exod. 24.9–11); whereas the Greek is: 'They saw the place where the God of Israel stands, and under his feet there was like a plinth of sapphire . . . *And not one of the chosen men of Israel was out of tune*, and they were seen in the place of God and ate and drank' (Lxx Exod. 24.9–11). 'Were seen' looks like a later 'correction' to avoid the idea of seeing God, as does the circumlocution 'the place of God'. But why the musical reference to being in harmony, unless this was the natural response to the vision? There is no basis for this in the MT.

Philo alludes to this harmony and reveals its context. By drawing on explanations scattered throughout his extensive works, it is possible to piece together something of the relationship between the music, the bonds of creation, the angels, the glory of God and the human mind seeking knowledge of these things. Scholars have been particularly puzzled by the bonds, as they can find no basis for them in Greek philosophy which is assumed to be the primary basis for Philo's thought and imagery.[91] In fact he was thinking as an educated Jew who knew temple tradition.

He describes the bonds as the angels spreading throughout creation to secure it, and this leads Philo to think of music.

---

[88] *2 Enoch* 2.5.
[89] *Ascension of Isaiah* 10.5.
[90] See above, p. 6.
[91] D. T. Runia, *Philo of Alexandria and the Timaeus of Plato*, Leiden: Brill, 1986, p. 240.

[The Maker] is everywhere because he has made his powers extend through earth and water, air and heaven, and left no part of the universe without his presence, and uniting all with all he has bound them fast with invisible bonds that they should never be loosed, and because of this I shall celebrate with song ... But this divine nature which presents itself to us, as visible and comprehensible and everywhere, is in reality invisisble, incomprehensible and nowhere.[92]

He goes on to speak of the angels as the choral dance in creation.

There is in the air a most holy choir, *choros*, of bodiless souls, attending on the heavenly powers, whom the sacred scriptures call angels. The whole army is drawn up in connected ranks to serve and minister to the leader who set them up in order, and, as is right and proper, to follow him as their Leader.[93]

The person who seeks the presence of God must join this angel music and dance.

[The human mind] is borne yet higher into the ether and into the circuit of heaven, and is whirled around with the dances of planets and fixed stars, in accordance with the laws of perfect music, following that love of wisdom that guides its steps ...[94]

Philo chose very similar words to describe the Therapeuts, whose name means 'healers' or 'worshippers', a monastic group of both men and women in northern Egypt. They cultivated their spiritual sight and wanted to 'soar above the sun of our senses' to the vision of the One Who Is. They wore white robes and used to spend much time singing hymns, sometimes in processions and sometimes in 'wheeling and counterwheeling of a choric dance'.[95] Eusebius said they were the earliest Christian communities (or maybe their forebears), a position that is usually dismissed nowadays. But Eusebius, a bishop writing in Palestine in the early fourth century CE, knew more about the early Christians than we do, and must have known that circular dances were part of early Christian worship.[96] Were they imitating Philo's

---

[92] Philo, *Tongues* 136–8.
[93] Philo, *Tongues* 174.
[94] Philo, *Creation* 70–1.
[95] Philo, *Contemplative Life* 11, 66, 84.
[96] Eusebius, *History* 2.17.

angels? Enoch had seen angels moving in this way: angels in white robes encircling the holy of holies, and Enoch was dazzled by the light.[97]

Philo also explained that enigmatic passage where Moses asked to see the face of God (Exod. 33.18–23). 'I beseech thee that I may at least see the glory that surrounds thee, and by thy glory I understand the powers that keep guard around thee.' Moses longed 'to have knowledge of them', that is, to learn about the angels. The LORD replied: 'The powers which thou seekest to know are discerned not by sight but by mind, even as I, whose powers they are, am discerned by mind and not by sight.'[98] Or, as Jesus said: 'Blessed are the pure in heart [i.e. mind], for they shall see God' (Matt. 5.8). Philo said this purity was expressed in silent hymns: '[Our gratitude to God] must be expressed by means of hymns of praise, and these not such as the audible voice shall sing, but strains raised and re-echoed by the mind too pure for eye to discern.'[99]

All the throne visions except Daniel's describe the music. When Isaiah saw the throne he heard the voices of the *seraphim* calling out, 'Holy, holy, holy is the LORD of Hosts; the whole earth is full of his glory.' When Enoch saw the throne he heard 'those who sleep not' – whom he distinguished from the archangels – singing 'Holy holy holy is the LORD of Spirits; filled with spirits is the earth.'[100] Where there is any detail, the song of the angels praises the Creator. The Sanctus in Isaiah proclaims the glory through the whole earth; the Sanctus in *1 Enoch* proclaims that the earth is full of spirits. The glory and the spirits are equivalents, as Philo's Moses knew: 'By thy glory I understand the powers that keep guard around thee . . .' Philo said they upheld and protected the creation: 'God is One, but he has around him powers without number which all assist and protect what has been created . . .'[101] Now in Christian liturgy, the Sanctus is set at the heart of the Eucharist, the Church's rite of atonement and covenant renewal, exactly where the song of the angels would have been in the temple.

---

[97] *1 Enoch* 71.1, 8.

[98] Philo, *Special Laws* I.45–6.

[99] Philo, *On Planting* 126.

[100] *1 Enoch* 39.12, translation by D. Olson, *Enoch* (North Richland Hills: Bibal Press, 2004).

[101] Philo *Tongues* 171.

When Ezekiel saw the throne he heard a sound like many waters, which he said was the sound of wings (Ezek. 1.24). John compared it to harps: 'I heard a voice from heaven like the sound of many waters, and like the sound of loud thunder; the voice I heard was like the sound of harpers playing on their harps, and they sing a new song before the throne . . .' (Rev. 14.2–3). Comparing the music to the sound of waters flowing may be another indication of the role of music in the vision of the throne. As we have seen, the throne was surrounded by fountains of righteousness and wisdom, and from it flowed the river of life.[102] Amos' criticism of temple music makes exactly this comparison:

> Take away from me the noise of your songs;
> To the melody of your harps I will not listen.
> But let justice, *mishpat*, roll down like waters,
> And righteousness, *tsᵉdāqāh*, like an ever-flowing stream.
>
> (Amos 5.23–24)

Waters and temple music is not an obvious comparison, unless there was a natural association within temple theology. Justice and righteousness were, however, an established pair: the LORD had looked for them as fruit in his vineyard (Isa. 5.7 – there are many other examples); and in his vision of the kingdom with wisdom restored, he presented justice and righteousness that had been *poured out* by the Spirit as the components of peace (Isa. 32.1–3, 15–17).

The music could have represented something coming from heaven to earth, and here we look at the slightly different version of Psalm 104 found at Qumran. The MT has:

> When thou hidest thy face, [all created things] are dismayed;
> When *thou takest away their Spirit*,[103] they die and return to dust.
> When thou sendest forth thy Spirit they are created;
> And thou renewest[104] the face of the ground . . .
>
> (Ps. 104.29–30)

The Qumran text is '. . . thou takest away *thy* Spirit . . .', implying that the life of all created things is the Spirit of the Creator.

---

[102] See above, p. 32.
[103] 'Spirit' and 'breath' are the same word in Hebrew.
[104] 'Renewed' here is the word that gives the 'new' song.

This was also the theme of Peter's sermon in the temple. No date is given for this sermon, but it was after Pentecost, and the next major temple festival was new year and day of atonement. Peter's theme was the day of atonement: 'Repent, therefore and turn again, that your sins may be blotted out, that times of refreshing may come from the presence of the LORD . . .' (Acts 3.19, my translation). 'You denied the Holy and Righteous One . . . you killed the Author of Life . . .' (Acts 3.14, 15). The LORD was the source of life.

Clement of Alexandria, and presumably other Christians too, knew the role of temple music which the Christians had kept. He contrasted the music of the Greek temples and the music of the Christians. The latter, he said, was 'the immortal measure of the new harmony which bears God's name – *the new Levitical song*'. This song drives out demons and brings creation to order.

> Behold the might of the new song! It has made men out of stones, men out of beasts. Those who were as dead because they did not partake of the true life, have come to life simply by becoming listeners to this song. It also composed the universe into melodious order, and tuned the discord of the elements into harmonious arrangement, so that the whole world might become harmony. It let loose the fluid ocean, and yet has prevented it from encroaching on the land. The earth again, which had been in a state of commotion, it has established and fixed the sea as its boundary.[105]

John's vision shows how the angel song was understood by the earliest Christians. He stood in the holy of holies and saw the throne with its thunder and lighting, the seven fiery spirits, the living creatures, the elders, and countless angels, all praising the one-who-sits-on-the-throne-and-the-Lamb.[106] The elders offered incense, which means they were priests (Rev. 5.8). John gave few details, but for him, the divine unity was full of heavenly beings in their various ranks. They sang the Sanctus and then, like Isaiah and Enoch, they linked the holiness to the power of the Creator, praising the One who had created all things. The extent of the worship changed when the Lamb was enthroned. At that point, the earth was included in the heavenly liturgy: 'Every creature in heaven and on earth and under

---

[105] *Exhortation to the Greeks* 1.
[106] See below, p. 104.

the earth and in the sea, and all therein . . .' (Rev. 5.13). Enthroning the Lamb meant that earth joined with heaven in the song of praise. Or perhaps we should say, earth joined with heaven *again* in the song of praise.

Stories told at that time said that the music of heaven had been lost through Adam's sin, and Christians believed that the incarnation of the Son of God had enabled the human race to hear again the song of the angels. This is why Luke described the shepherds at Bethlehem hearing angel music when Jesus was born: 'Glory to God in the highest and on earth peace . . .' (Luke 2.14). These very familiar words show the role of angel music: praising God in heaven brings peace on earth. Adam had heard the song of the *seraphim* – 'Holy holy holy' – when he was in Paradise, before he sinned: 'But after I transgressed against the law, I no longer heard that sound.'[107] This tradition is found in the *Testament of Adam*, a Jewish text preserved and expanded by the early Christians. It lists the praises of all creation in order, each rank having its appointed hour to worship: heavenly beings, weathers, plants, birds, animals and, at the last hour of the day, human beings.

The Qumran *Community Rule* shows that they also attuned their worship to the pattern of creation and the 'engraved laws' of the Creator.

> I will sing praise with knowledge, and all my music [will be]
>   for the glory of God.
> My harp and my lute to mark the measure of his holiness,
> And the pipe of my lips I shall raise up to his just order.
> When day and night come, I will enter into the covenant of
>   God,
> And when evening and morning go out, I will recount his
>   statutes.[108]

'Knowledge' and 'music' suggest that the covenant and decrees were not the Mosaic covenant and the Ten Commandments, but rather the everlasting covenant and the 'engraved statutes' for the creation.[109] The hymn continues with reference to the source of knowledge,

---

[107] *Testament of Adam* 1.4.
[108] *Community Rule*, 1QS X.9–10.
[109] We shall return to this. See below, pp. 121–2.

the *raz nihyeh*, concealed wisdom and knowledge, and gazing on the eternal.

Restoring the angel music and what it represented remained important in the Church. Three great theologians from the fourth century CE show that the detail was not lost:

- John Chrysostom, expounding Isaiah's vision, said: 'Above, the hosts of angels sing praise. Below, men form choirs in the church and imitate them by singing the same doxology.'[110]
- Basil of Caesarea was still using the word 'chorus': 'What is more blessed than to imitate here on earth the chorus of angels?'[111]
- Gregory of Nyssa preached a Christmas sermon using verses from the psalm for Tabernacles (Ps. 118.24, 26, 27) and drew on the ancient themes. The LORD, he said, had come to restore the original unity of all creation, which was 'the temple of the LORD of creation'. The sound of praise in that temple had ceased through sin, but as a result of the Incarnation, when the LORD appeared, the human creation was able to sing again in the great liturgy of heaven and earth, joining together in a choral dance, as they had formerly done. 'Let us direct our souls to the spiritual chorus. Let us have David as [the leader of] our choir, and together with him let us send forth the sweet sound which we once sang.'[112]

Dionysius, too, the influential and undatable theologian with whom we began this chapter, said that Isaiah was taught the song of the angels in order to learn the heavenly knowledge. 'He was also introduced to the mystery of that divine and much honoured hymnody, for the angel of his vision taught the theologian [i.e. Isaiah], as far as possible, whatever he knew himself of the sacred.'[113]

Within living memory of the first generation, as we have seen, Clement could write in Rome:

> Think of the vast company of angels, who all wait on him to serve his wishes. 'Ten thousand times ten thousand stood before him', says Scripture, 'and thousand thousands did him service, crying, "Holy,

---

[110] John Chrysostom, *Homily on Isaiah* 6, in Migne, *Patrologia Greco-Latina*, LVI.97.

[111] Basil of Caesarea, *Letter I.2*, in Migne, *Patrologia Greco-Latina*, XXXII.225.

[112] Gregory of Nyssa, *Christmas Sermon*, in Migne, *Patrologia Greco-Latina*, XLVI 1127–8. I do not know of an English version.

[113] Dionysius, *Celestial Hierarchy* 305A.

holy Holy is the LORD of hosts; all creation is full of his glory." ' In the same way ought we ourselves, gathered together *in a conscious unity, to cry to him as it were with a single voice*, if we are to obtain a share of his glorious promises.[114]

The angel music and the theology it represented have been largely overlooked by recent scholarship because of the influence of Deuteronomy. The key elements of the angel music and its meaning – the vision of God, the throne, the hosts, the music and calling the LORD to the temple, atonement – are all missing from the Deuteronomic writings. Their account of Moses receiving the commandments denies that the LORD was seen (Deut. 4.12); their description of the temple in 1 Kings says nothing of the throne (cf. 1 Chron. 28.18); they say nothing of the Levites and their music; they denied that the LORD could dwell in the temple (1 Kings 8.27); they removed the 'Hosts' from the title LORD of Hosts (Isa. 37.16, cf. 2 Kings 19.15); there was no day of atonement in their calendar (Deut. 16); and they denied that anyone could make atonement for the sins of Israel (Exod. 32.31–33). The early Christians, on the other hand, kept all these things and they worshipped like the Levites. With their music they praised the LORD, they gave thanks ('eucharist') and they called on the LORD to come – which is what *Maranatha* means.

The earliest glimpse of their worship is John's vision of heaven where the heavenly beings clustered around the throne and worshipped: 'For thou didst create all things, and by thy will they existed and were created' (Rev. 4.11). Later temple mystics said they had actually been created from the engravings on the throne. The throne, as we shall see, symbolized the Lady of the temple – Wisdom – someone almost lost to contemporary readings of the Bible, due to its translators and interpreters. The correcting scribes are not just a phenomenon of the remote past. The angels from the throne were called the children of Wisdom.

***

The early Christians not only knew about the angels of the older temple tradition, they lived in their world. Even a brief overview such as this shows that the early Church kept the angel lore, which shaped

---

[114] *1 Clement* 34.

both its liturgy and its way of life. Evidence in contemporary and later sources – the Gnostics, the *merkavah* mystics – shows that they all had a common root in the original temple, and that similarity to the teaching of Pythagoras, especially as this passed into Platonism, could also be due to temple influence. The world of Dionysius, with which we began, may well owe less to Greek influences than is often assumed by the pupils of the correcting scribes, and more to temple mysticism which is rarely even considered.

4

The throne

The focus of temple mysticism was the divine throne. The 'golden chariot of the cherubim that spread their wings and covered the ark of the covenant of the LORD' stood in the holy of holies in Solomon's temple (1 Chron. 28.18). Nobody knows exactly what the *cherubim* looked like. There are examples of thrones from Phoenicia and Canaan[1] made from two animals with human faces, their back-swept wings forming the arms of the throne. The king sat between the creatures. The *cherubim* in the temple, however, had outstretched wings that reached, wingtip to wingtip, right across the holy of holies. Each had a wingspan of five metres, an enormous throne if it was like those of Canaan and Phoenicia. Ezekiel saw the throne leaving the temple, but his visionary experience left him bewildered and this is reflected in the description. The four *cherubim* he saw were the same as the four living creatures, said his editor (Ezek. 10.20), so this throne had four *cherubim*, not two; and each had four wings: two stretched out towards another *cherub* and two covering its body (Ezek. 1.23). The throne was *above* them, not between them. They supported the 'awesome crystal'[2] firmament, on which was a sapphire throne (Ezek. 1.26). Two *cherubim* or four is an unsolved problem, as is their precise relationship to the living creatures. John did not mention *cherubim* with the throne, only the living creatures (Rev. 4.6–7; 5.6–14).

'Enthroned on the *cherubim*' was a title for the LORD. Hezekiah prayed: 'O LORD of Hosts, God of Israel, who art enthroned on the cherubim . . .' (Isa. 37.16), and the psalmist called on the One on the *cherubim* to shine forth (Ps. 80.2; also Ps. 99.1). Although now associated with the temple, the title was used in the stories of Samuel and David (1 Sam. 4.4; 2 Sam. 6.2; 1 Chron. 13.6); and so thought to be in use before the temple was built. 'David' sang of the LORD

---

[1] Carved pictures found at Byblos and Megiddo.
[2] The literal meaning of the Hebrew.

flying on a *cherub*, 'seen on wings of wind/spirit' (2 Sam. 22.11 = Ps. 18.11[3]). In the Pentateuch, the LORD said he would appear between the *cherubim* over the ark to speak to Moses: 'From above the *kapporet*,[4] from between the two cherubim that are upon the ark . . . I will speak with you . . .' (Exod. 25.22); and he would appear to Aaron in the incense cloud over the *kapporet* (Lev. 16.2). The throne had been central to Israel's worship from the earliest times.

Although the throne was always associated with the *cherubim*, the meaning of *cherub* is uncertain: 'gracious' and 'mighty' have been suggested, on the basis of similarity to words in Aramaic and Assyrian respectively, but the most intriguing suggestion is found in Philo. 'The two winged creatures [over the ark], which in the Hebrew are called cherubim, we should term "full knowledge and much science"', *epignōsis kai epistēmē pollē*.[5] They represented 'knowledge poured out in abundance'.[6] This has been dismissed as a fanciful suggestion by Philo – there is no basis for this meaning in the Hebrew word – but there must have been a reason for what he said. He also said that the two *cherubim* represented the two aspects/powers of the LORD, the creative and the royal.[7] Philo, then, associated the *cherubim* with the highest manifestation of the powers that collectively were the LORD, and with knowledge poured out. The pouring out of knowledge (or wisdom) from the holy of holies is something we have met before, so maybe Philo knew that the *cherub* throne was associated with knowledge. He knew, as we have seen, that 'Israel' meant the man who looks on God, and even though the etymology he offered is also considered dubious,[8] there is abundant evidence that 'the man who sees God' was an important feature of the older faith. Philo knew about temple mysticism, even though much of what he said has been identified as something he borrowed from the Greek mystery cults.

By the end of the second temple period, the holy of holies was empty. The *cherub* throne had gone. Josephus wrote: 'The innermost

---

[3] The wording is slightly different in the Psalm.
[4] Usually translated 'mercy seat'.
[5] Philo, *Moses* II 97.
[6] Philo, *Questions on Exodus* II.62.
[7] Philo, *Questions on Exodus* II.62.
[8] See above, p. 59.

part was twenty cubits, screened . . . from the outer part by a veil. In it was nothing at all. It was not to be entered, nor defiled, nor seen.'[9] This prompts two questions: why, if the holy of holies that they knew was empty, did the mystics in the time of Jesus describe a place where there were angels and a chariot throne? Presumably because their tradition originated before the holy of holies was empty. And why did people long for the return of the temple furnishings? It was still said, long after the second temple had been destroyed, that in the time of the Messiah the furnishings missing from the second temple would be restored: the ark, the fire, the *cherubim*, the Spirit and the menorah. These had been 'hidden away' in the time of Josiah, *and all except the menorah had belonged in the holy of holies*. Since there was a menorah in the second temple,[10] the one to be restored must have been in some way different. Perhaps the true menorah had also stood in the holy of holies rather than in the great hall of the temple.[11] It was restored to the holy of holies in John's vision of the tree of life and the throne (Rev. 22.1–5).

Add to this the fact that the Deuteronomists' account of the temple does not mention the *cherub* throne, but does mention Josiah burning a chariot of the sun[12] when he purged the temple. A tree-like object (? the true menorah) was the real focus of his anger, and it was treated with particular fury (2 Kings 23.6). He also removed the cult of angels from the temple,[13] along with the anointing oil.[14] The Deuteronomists who prompted Josiah's temple purges suppressed so much of what we now recognize as temple mysticism. They denied that the vision of God was possible and they offered their Law as the substitute for Wisdom, as we have seen. The Enoch tradition remembered that Wisdom had been abandoned at this time, and that the temple priests lost their vision;[15] and it was shortly after this that

---

[9] Josephus, *War* 5.219.

[10] The Romans took it as loot, as can be seen on the arch of Titus.

[11] This is implied by Exodus 40.24, which describes the position of the menorah in the tabernacle.

[12] The Hebrew is plural, chariots, but the Greek is singular, which could suggest that the correcting scribes had been at work on the Hebrew.

[13] The word translated 'cult prostitutes', 2 Kings 23.7, has the same consonants as 'holy ones', angels: *qᵉdēshim*, prostitutes; *qᵉdōshim*, holy ones.

[14] Babylonian Talmud *Horayoth* 12a.

[15] *1 Enoch* 93.8.

Ezekiel saw the chariot throne leave the temple, along with the fire and the Spirit.[16]

There can be no proof, but all this evidence suggests that the older faith, centred on the holy of holies and the throne, the Lady and her Son, the LORD, was driven out by Josiah. The lost furnishings of the temple – the ark, the fire, the *cherubim*, the Spirit and the menorah, together with the anointing oil – were all symbols of the Lady. The older faith survived in the memories and teachings of the temple mystics and their heirs: the devotees of the *merkavah* and the Christians. The Qumran Melchizedek text looked for the return of 'teachers who had been kept hidden and secret'[17] – who were they? – and Psalm 110, the Melchizedek psalm, is a much used text in the New Testament but also one of the most damaged passages in the Hebrew scriptures. It describes the birth of a Melchizedek figure in the holy of holies, someone who was invited to sit on the throne and was the divine Son. Jesus was proclaimed as this 'Melchizedek' (Heb. 7.11), which may explain why parts of the Melchizedek psalm are now opaque. Mary was proclaimed as his heavenly Mother, and the throne was remembered as her symbol.

We now look at three ways in which the throne was important in temple mysticism:

- how those who sat on the throne were reborn and lived the life of heaven: they were equal to angels, sons of God, sons of the resurrection (Luke 20.36);
- how there were heavenly archetypes of all creation engraved on the throne;
- how those who stood by the throne looked out at creation with new eyes and learned that all creation was one.

Born from above

John took several themes from temple mysticism to show how far the Jews had lost touch with their original temple teachings, and the

---

[16] See below, pp. 110–11.

[17] 11Q Melchizedek. This is the translation in F. Garcia-Martinez, ed., *Discoveries in the Judean Desert* XXIII, Oxford: Oxford University Press, 1998, p. 229. G. Vermes, *The Complete Dead Sea Scrolls in English*, London: Penguin, 1997, renders the words 'he will assign them to the sons of heaven'.

first of these was being born from above/born again. Josephus, his contemporary, defined 'the Jews' as people who had returned from Babylon,[18] which means they were the heirs of those who had purged the temple and rejected the older ways. It is likely that John used the term in the same way. The 'Jews', he implied throughout his Gospel, no longer understood their own heritage. They did not understand that the Sabbath signified the rest at the completion of the creation, the great 'tomorrow' that became central to the Christian vision (John 5.6–18); they had lost the original meaning of their scriptures, which showed the LORD in human form (John 5.39; 8.39–41); they did not understand the ancient belief in ascent to heaven (John 6.41–42; 7.35–36; 8.22); or what it meant to be Son of God (John 10.34–39). There are many examples, the first being Jesus' meeting with Nicodemus, who did not understand what it meant to be born again. 'How can a man be born when he is old? Can he enter a second time into his mother's womb and be born?' Jesus then taught him about birth 'from above' and seeing the kingdom of God, being born of water and the Spirit and entering the kingdom of God (John 3.3–8). This was the mystery of the temple, and yet Jesus had to say to Nicodemus: 'Are you the teacher in Israel and yet you do not understand this?' (John 3.10, my translation).

The key passage for understanding 'birth from above' is Psalm 110.3. The psalm is addressed by the LORD to another whom the psalmist calls 'my Lord'. 'Sit at my right hand, till I make your enemies your footstool.' This was the LORD speaking to the Davidic king, inviting him to share the throne. The king was promised triumph over his enemies, as in Psalm 2: 'Serve the LORD with fear, and rejoice with trembling, kiss the son . . .' (Ps. 2.11–12, AV, which translates literally); or Psalm 89: 'I will crush his foes before him and strike down those who hate him' (Ps. 89.23). Psalm 2 also says that the king was 'born': 'You are my son, today I have begotten you' (Ps. 2.7); and Psalm 89 says that he was raised up and anointed: 'I have exalted one chosen from the people . . . with my holy oil I have anointed him' (Ps. 89.19–20). The Hebrew text of Psalm 110 does

---

[18] Josephus, *Antiquities* 11.173. The Samaritans claimed to be 'Hebrews but not Jews', *Antiquities* 11.344.

not, apparently, mention either the birth or the anointing of the king, but both are/were there, before the correcting scribes did their work. What has been obscured is a fundamental aspect of temple mysticism and the key to understanding what the Christians meant by 'Son of God'.

The crucial verse is: 'Your people will offer themselves freely on the day you lead your host upon the holy mountains. From the womb of the morning like dew your youth will come to you' (Ps. 110.3). This cannot honestly be called a translation, since all the words but 'day' and 'dew' are uncertain. Not all the discussion, however, is relevant to an introduction to temple mysticism. 'On the day you lead your host' was probably once 'on the day of your birth', since the Hebrew words for 'army/host' and 'birth' look similar. 'Upon the holy mountains' could formerly have been 'in the beauties of holiness' (thus AV), since 'mountains', *hrry*, and 'beauties' *hdry*, differ by one letter, and those two letters look similar; or they could have been 'in the chambers of the holy ones', since 'chambers', *ḥdry*, also differs by one similar-looking letter. 'Your youth will come to you', *yalduteyka*, is written with exactly the same letters as 'I have begotten you', *y*e*lidtiyka*;[19] and 'dew' was a well-known image for the anointing oil, e.g. Psalm 133.2–3. This, then, was the heavenly birth and anointing of the king, and birth into the life of heaven was what they meant by resurrection. 'From the womb of the morning' is opaque: 'morning', *sh*e*har*, means 'dawn' but it was also the name for the morning star in the pantheon of neighbouring Ugarit. The Morning Star was the son of their great sun goddess, one of whose names was Rahmay, the same as the Hebrew word here translated 'womb'; and Morning Star was a title given to their crown prince who was the 'son' of the sun goddess. It was also a title given to Jesus: 'the offspring of David, the bright Morning Star' (Rev. 22.16), showing that this aspect of the ancient Davidic tradition was known to the early Christians.

Psalm 110 describes what happened in the holy of holies as the human king became the divine Son, which did not mean *the son of Yahweh* but rather the manifestation of Yahweh in a human. This was both the incarnation of the LORD and also the adoption of the

---

[19] The Lxx has 'I have begotten you'.

human king as the divine Son, his *theosis*. Many terms have been invented to try to describe the relationship between the human and the divine in Jesus, but the origin is described here in this mutilated psalm. The human king entered the holy of holies – 'the beauty of holiness/the chambers of the holy ones'; he was anointed with 'dew', which in temple practice was the sacrament of resurrection, and then enthroned – 'sit at my right hand'. Some early Christians naturally read this verse as a prophecy of the birth of Jesus; by changing one letter, they made 'womb' into 'Mary': 'I have begotten you as the Morning Star from Mary'.[20]

Sitting on the throne was the moment of his birth as Son of God. In temple discourse, the Messiah was by definition both Son of God and resurrected; he was the risen LORD. The Chronicler's account of Solomon's coronation does say that the king became the LORD at his enthronement, but the English translations 'correct' the text and thus obscure important evidence: *Solomon sat on the throne of the LORD as king* (1 Chron. 29.23). 'Then David said to all the assembly, "Bless the LORD your God." And all the assembly blessed the LORD, the God of their fathers, and bowed their heads and worshipped the LORD, the king' (1 Chron. 29.20, translating literally). Several English versions insert an extra verb, and have 'they worshipped the LORD *and* did obeisance to the king' as though these were separate acts. The Hebrew has only one verb but two objects: they worshipped the LORD and the king. The union of divine and human was expressed in this way, the divine first and then the human: 'the-LORD-and-the-king' or 'God-and-the-Lamb'. This latter and similar expressions are frequently found in Revelation.

The uniting of divine and human is the key to understanding the enthronement scene in Revelation. The (human) Lamb became divine when he was seated on the throne, just as Solomon did. An early Christian hymn assumes the same scene, saying that the human being was given the Name, that is, given the name Yahweh, the LORD, and was then worshipped by all creation.

---

[20] Eusebius, *Commentary on the Psalms*, Migne, *Patrologia Greco-Latina*, XXIII 1344. I do not know of an English version. Eusebius implies that they read *mrḥm*, from the womb, as *mrym*, Mary. This also implies they were using the archaic Hebrew script, where the two letters look similar.

God has highly exalted him and bestowed on him the Name that
is above every name, that at the name of Jesus [i.e. the LORD, the
name he now bears] every knee should bow in heaven and on
earth and under the earth, and every tongue confess that Jesus Christ
is the LORD, to the glory of God the Father.

(Phil. 2.9–11, my translation)

There are very few examples of early Christian hymns, so it is interesting that two – this one and the heavenly hymn in Revelation 5 – both
assume the same setting.

Receiving the Name was the same as sitting on the throne and
receiving the scroll. The scene John described – the Lamb enthroned
and then receiving the worship of all creation – is one of the mysteries
of the temple. It is often stated and alluded to, but never explained.
Moses, according to Philo, was named God and King when he entered
the darkness where God was, 'the unseen, invisible, incorporeal
and archetypal essence of existing things. Thus he beheld what is
hidden from the sight of mortal nature . . .'[21] He had entered the state
represented by the holy of holies, but in Moses' case it was the cloud
on Sinai. We shall return to this.[22]

In the remainder of his vision John refers to a single being: 'he-
who-sits-upon-the-throne-and-the-Lamb' (Rev. 5.13, my translation);
'the throne of God-and-the-Lamb' (Rev. 22.3, my translation), followed
by 'and they shall worship *him*', singular, not *them*; 'Salvation belongs
to our God who sits upon the throne, and to the Lamb', and they
worshipped God – no mention of the Lamb (Rev. 7.10–11; similarly
at 11.15 and 20.6). Some early versions of Revelation have 'the day
of *his* wrath' rather than 'the day of *their* wrath' (Rev. 6.17), and one
can see why there was confusion. At the heart of the holy of holies,
and so of creation, was a human enthroned, and certain people
knew that they had become that person: Jesus said he had been with
the living creatures and the angels served him (Mark 1.13), so he
knew he was the LORD. Someone who had the same experience
left his words at Qumran: 'a throne of strength in the assembly of
the *'ēlim* . . . my glory is [incomparable], and apart from me none
is exalted. I am reckoned with the *'ēlim* and I dwell in the holy

---

[21] Philo, *Moses* I.158.
[22] See below, Chapter 5.

assembly . . . I am reckoned with the *'ēlim* and my glory is with the sons of the King . . .'[23]

Two early Christian texts show how this temple birth was remembered. The *Infancy Gospel of James* presents the cave of the Nativity as the holy of holies and the moment of birth as a bright cloud coming with a great light, just as the glory filled the tabernacle and the temple (Exod. 40.34–35; 1 Kings 8.10–11).

> [Joseph and the midwife] stood by the cave and there was a bright cloud overshadowing it . . . Immediately the cloud withdrew from the cave and a light appeared there, so great that we could not look at it. Gradually the light withdrew until the young child appeared . . .[24]

The *Gospel of Philip*, one of the Nag Hammadi texts, described the holy of holies as 'the bridal chamber', the place of divine light, and a great fire appearing at the birth. The language is enigmatic, and the punctuation uncertain, but the gist is clear.

> The Father of everything united with the virgin who came down and a fire shone for him on that day. He appeared in the great bridal chamber. Therefore his body came into being on that very day. It left the bridal chamber as one who came into being from the bridegroom and the bride . . .
>
> The mysteries of this marriage are perfected rather in the day and in the light. Neither that day nor its light ever sets. If anyone becomes a son of the bridal chamber, he will receive the light.[25]

The new-born king was a 'priest for ever after the order of Melchi-Zedek' (Ps. 110.4, my translation). 'After the order of' is a problem, as we shall see,[26] but Melchi-Zedek was usually written as two words, suggesting it was a title rather than a name: the king of righteousness, or the righteous king. The only other reference to Melchizedek in the Hebrew scriptures is where he brought Abram bread and wine and blessed him. He was priest of God Most High, but who was Melchizedek and who was his God? It is only the post-Christian Hebrew text of

---

[23] 4Q491 fr. 11.
[24] *Infancy Gospel of James* 19.
[25] *Gospel of Philip* 71, 86.
[26] See below, p. 120.

105

Genesis and works dependent on it[27] that name Melchizedek's God as 'the LORD God Most High', that is, name his God as Yahweh (Gen. 14.18–24). The other ancient texts and versions say simply 'God Most High', implying that Melchi-Zedek was himself the LORD, and that his meeting with Abram was a theophany.

One of the ancient texts was the *Apocalypse of Abraham*, which retells what happened after Abram met Melchi-Zedek. Genesis says the LORD appeared to Abram in a vision (Gen. 15.1–21); the *Apocalypse* says Abram met the angel Yahweh-el, who was dressed as a high priest.[28] This angel was probably Melchi-Zedek the priest of God Most High, implying that *Melchi-Zedek was the name for the LORD in human form as the royal high priest*. This is what Psalm 110 implies, and also the Qumran Melchizedek text in which texts about the LORD are applied to Melchizedek.[29] In Hebrews, Jesus is identified as Melchi-Zedek, and his priesthood contrasted with Aaron's. Aaron's sons became priests by descent – their priesthood was hereditary and ended when they died – whereas a Melchizedek priest became so by ascent, he was 'raised up' – the word for resurrection – and did not die. Melchizedek was a priest 'not according to . . . bodily descent but by the power of an indestructible life' (Heb. 7.11, 15, 16). Here, then, is the resurrected figure of Psalm 110, the human who became Yahweh with his people, and here we see why the correcting scribes changed the name of Melchizedek's God. As a priest of Yahweh-God-Most-High, Melchizedek could not have been Yahweh in human form, which is what the Christians were claiming for Jesus, their Melchizedek.

Isaiah gave a series of oracles about the heavenly birth of the Davidic king, this Melchizedek figure, and the Christians recognized them as prophecies of Jesus. They originally referred to the actual heir to the throne, oracles of assurance that the dynasty would survive the current crisis, and there would be another Davidic king. The Virgin who would give birth to Immanuel (Isa. 7.14) was the Lady of the temple, and, as at Ugarit, she was deemed the heavenly mother of the royal child who would one day become the LORD, the king. The great Isaiah scroll from Qumran has one different letter in this

---

[27] Such as the Targums.
[28] *Apocalypse of Abraham* 10.1—11.6.
[29] 11QMelchizedek.

106

oracle which reveals exactly who 'the Virgin' was. The words to Ahaz, according to the MT, were 'Ask a sign of the LORD your God', but according to the older Qumran text, they were 'Ask a sign of the *Mother* of the LORD your God'. The LORD was the Son of God Most High, and the Virgin was his mother.

One of the Lady's titles was Wisdom, and so her son became the emissary/angel(s) of wisdom, as can be seen in the second of Isaiah's oracles. The angels sing in the holy of holies: 'Unto us a child is born, unto us a son is given . . .' and they give the royal child his throne names (Isa. 9.6). The Hebrew text has four – Wonderful Counsellor, Mighty God, Everlasting Father, Prince of Peace – but the Greek summarized them as 'the Angel of Great Counsel. The four were one, as with the archangels.'[30] Isaiah's third oracle describes the anointing, when the human king received the manifold Spirit of the LORD which transformed his thinking and knowing. This was the sign of the temple mystic.

> The Spirit of the LORD shall rest upon him,
> The spirit of wisdom and understanding,
> The spirit of counsel and might,
> The spirit of knowledge and the fear of the LORD.
>
> (Isa. 11.2)

The result was a person who no longer formed judgements with his own senses, but filled the earth with the knowledge of the LORD (Isa. 11.3, 9). 'His delight shall be in the fear of the LORD' is, literally, 'His perfume shall be the fear of the LORD', showing that the Spirit was given through the perfumed anointing oil (Isa. 11.3).

This kingmaking passed into the Christians' way of describing Jesus. John saw the Lamb (meaning a human figure), standing (meaning resurrected), *even though* it had been slain. He was interpreting the resurrection and death of Jesus in terms of the temple mystery. The Lamb was in the midst of the throne (meaning he was enthroned), and he had the seven spirits and seven eyes (meaning he had the totality of the divine Spirit). The rest of the kingmaking followed. He was given the sealed scroll to open (he was given secret

---

[30] See above, p. 67. Jesus spoke of the children of Wisdom (Luke 7.35) and of Wisdom sending the prophets (Luke 11.49), who would also have been described as children of Wisdom.

knowledge). A similar ceremony is described for the boy king Joash: he was crowned, given the testimony – whatever that was – made king, anointed and then acclaimed (2 Kings 11.12).

The ritual in the holy of holies meant that the king was 'resurrected' and born as a divine Son at the start of his reign. This was also true of Jesus, who was 'resurrected' at his baptism when he was proclaimed as the Son. It is curious that the New Testament never uses the post-mortem resurrection texts of Jesus, texts such as Isaiah 26.19: 'Thy dead shall live, their bodies shall rise' or the dry bones of Ezekiel 37, or even Daniel 12.2: 'Many of those who sleep in the dust of the earth shall awake.' Instead, the Christians proclaimed that Jesus fulfilled the royal 'ascent' texts, showing that they understood Jesus' resurrection in the temple sense. They quoted the song of the Servant who suffered, was raised up and was given knowledge (Isa. 52.13—53.12); they quoted the promise to the new king, 'Today I have begotten you' (Ps. 2.7, quoted at Jesus' baptism in the oldest version of Luke 3.22); and they quoted the Melchizedek texts.

If Jesus' baptism was the moment of his throne experience, it would explain hints in early tradition that this was a *merkavah* experience.[31] The New Testament says Jesus saw the heavens open and felt the Spirit coming upon him – his anointing. Origen, the greatest biblical scholar of the early Church, said that Jesus saw what Ezekiel saw: the chariot throne.[32] The days that followed were his *merkavah* experience: Jesus was with the living creatures and the angels served him, in other words, he felt he had been enthroned as the LORD, the Son. The devil tempted him not to believe that he was the Son,[33] but John's Jesus knew he had been consecrated and sent into the world as the Son (John 10.36).

Jesus' resurrection at his baptism would explain the earliest Christian baptismal practice. In the old Syrian rite the newly baptized Christian emerged from the water as a 'son of God' and 'a son of light', and the font was called the womb.[34] The resurrection state began with baptism, and the question is: Was this rite drawn from Jesus' own

---

[31] The fire in the water of the Jordan, Origen teaching that Jesus saw what Ezekiel saw.

[32] Origen, *On Ezekiel*, Homily 1.4–7.

[33] See above, pp. 101–2.

[34] See my book *The Risen LORD*, Edinburgh: T&T Clark, 1996, pp. 27–55 for detail and references.

experience of sonship and resurrection at his baptism? The *Gospel of Philip* has a saying that makes best sense in this context:

> Those who say that the LORD died first and then rose up are in error, for he rose up first and then died. If one does not first attain the resurrection, will he not die? As God lives, he would be already [dead].[35]

Resurrection at baptism would also explain the early creed quoted by Paul: '[The Son] descended from David according to the flesh and designated Son of God in power according to the Spirit of holiness by his resurrection from the dead' (Rom. 1.3–4). Getting behind the awkward Greek to the Semitic original, this creed declares that Jesus was empowered as Son of God by the Holy Spirit when he rose from the dead. Now the only time the Spirit spoke to Jesus and designated him her son was at his baptism, and that is exactly how the Hebrew Christians told the story of his baptism.[36] 'You are my beloved son, with you I am well pleased' were, they said, the words of his mother the Holy Spirit, and when the Spirit came on him, he was resurrected in the temple mystics' sense of that word.

The throne had played an important part in the royal 'birth' rituals of Egypt, and it may be that Jerusalem practised something similar. The throne represented Isis the great goddess; she wore a throne as her headdress, and the throne was the hieroglyph of her name. 'There is excellent evidence that the great goddess Isis was originally the deified throne ... The prince who takes his seat upon it arises a king. Hence the throne is called the "mother" of the king',[37] and the Pharaoh was her son. When the king sat on the throne, he was seated on the lap of the goddess, an image familiar from later representations of Mary holding her Child. It is not possible to say that the Lady of the Jerusalem temple was the personification of the throne or that the throne was her symbol. What is beyond doubt is that when Ezekiel described the chariot throne leaving Jerusalem, he described the departure of a *female figure* on whom the glory of the LORD was enthroned.

---

[35] *Gospel of Philip*, CG II.3.56. 'Dead' is not clear in the text.
[36] Jerome, commenting on Isaiah 11.2, quoted this from the (now lost) *Gospel of the Hebrews*.
[37] H. Frankfort, *Before Philosophy*, London: Pelican, 1949, p. 26.

To find the Lady as the throne, we must look closely at the Hebrew text of Ezekiel, which has many rare words and many that could have several meanings. The Lady is not obvious in the English translations because the translators were not expecting to find her and, when they had to choose between several possibilities for difficult words, they did so knowing what the text ought to say. In the accounts of Ezekiel's visions (Ezek. 1 and 10), there is a curious confusion of singular and plural forms, and of masculine and feminine. In the AV, which is usually the most literal translation, there is: 'And the cherubims [masc.] were lifted up, this is the living creature [fem.] that I saw by the river of Chebar.' 'This is the living creature that I saw under the God of Israel by the river of Chebar; and I knew that they were the cherubims' (Ezek. 10.15, 20). When the *cherubim* moved, so did the Living Creature, 'for the spirit of the living creature was in them' (Ezek. 10.17). The 'living creature' is *ḥayyah*, a feminine noun which means a living thing or an animal, but also revival, new life, as in 'You found *new life* for your strength . . .' (Isa. 57.10). Translating *ḥayyah* as 'Living One' or even as 'Life Giver' makes Ezekiel's vision very interesting indeed. Her name appears in both singular and plural forms: the singular is found at Ezekiel 1.20, 21, 22 and at 10.15, 17, 20. The AV distinguishes between singular and plural, other versions do not.[38] The Life Giver seems to be the throne, and her name in both singular and plural forms suggests that she was divine.

Ezekiel described the throne he knew and it was alive. Much of the account is difficult to follow even in the Hebrew, and much more is lost in translation. There are, for example, two words for 'wheel': one, *'ōphan*, only means a wheel, but the other, *galgal*, can mean various round things including a whirling or a whirling wind. All the wheels in Ezekiel 1 are 'wheels' but in chapter 10 there are also 'whirlings' in vv. 2, 6, 13: 'Go in among the whirling underneath the cherub [sing.], and fill your hands with burning coals from between the cherubim [pl.] . . .' (Ezek. 10.2, my translation). In addition to the regular wheels of the chariot throne, Ezekiel described a whirling at its base. Each of the regular wheels was sparkling yellow, and

---

[38] Modern versions, e.g. the RSV and the NEB, do not distinguish singular and plural, and the JB is inconsistent, naming her the 'animal/animals' in chapter 1 and the 'creature' in chapter 10. 'Wisdom' also appears as a singular or a plural name; 'she' is plural in Proverbs 1.20; 9.1; 24.7.

each was 'a wheel within a wheel', if that is what the words mean (Ezek. 10.9–10). There have been ingenious suggestions such as the wheels intersecting at right angles (thus the GNB), but the line could mean there were concentric circles of yellow light. Ezekiel described several times the curious movement of the throne: it went straight forward without turning (Ezek. 1.9, 12), but could go straight in any of the four directions (Ezek. 1.17; 10.11).

There is a problem with almost every word in Ezekiel 10.12, which is a major part of the description of the throne. One suggestion is: '*And their whole body, and their backs, and their hands, and their wings*, and the wheels, were full of eyes round about, even the wheels that they four had' (Ezek. 10.12, AV). Many translations are offered for the words in italics: 'their bodies, their backs, their hands, their wings' (JB) is fairly close and the NEB and GNB are similar; 'their rims, and their spokes' (RSV) is very different. That piece of text may be lost to us. Then the word 'eye' can also mean 'point of light'; and the letters translated 'whole body' usually mean 'all flesh', as in 'All flesh shall see . . .' (Ezek. 20.48; 21.4, 5); or, in the story of Noah, 'I will . . . destroy all flesh in which is the breath of life', 'every living thing of all flesh . . .' (Gen. 6.17, 19). If this was a vision of the Living One, then it would not be surprising to find, within/around her, points of light that 'were' living things. A later *merkavah* text describes the spirits of the righteous by the throne of glory, those who have already been created and returned, and those still waiting to be created. There was a storehouse for souls by the throne, all of which had been created together and were waiting to enter the material world.[39] Rather nearer in time to Ezekiel are Moses' vision on Sinai as described in *Jubilees*, where he saw all the angels created in Day One, along with 'all the spirits of his creatures in heaven and on earth';[40] and Ben Sira's saying, 'He who lives in eternity created all things at the same time',[41] implying that everything was in some sense created in the holy of holies before it had a material existence.

It seems that Ezekiel knew the throne as the Living One(s), who was or was within the fourfold *cherub(im)*. She had a sapphire throne above her and a fiery whirling beneath. Around her were the souls

[39] *3 Enoch* 43.

[40] *Jubilees* 2.2.

[41] Ben Sira 18.1: 'at the same time' is *koine* in Lxx and *simul* in Vulgate.

of all living things, which Ezekiel saw as points of light, and she/they moved only in a straight line, but in any direction. There is nothing like this in the rest of the Hebrew scriptures, but there is something remarkably similar in the teachings attributed to Pythagoras, and to his followers Philolaus and Timaeus who lived in the late fifth century BCE, some two centuries after Ezekiel. Philolaus associated feminine divinities with the square, a curious idea but one which scholars recognize as deep rooted in Pythagorean teaching, and the most ancient sources show that Pythagoras was associated with the Great Mother mysteries.[42] His followers invoked the *tetraktys* (the fourness) as their most sacred oath, which was represented by 4:3:2:1 set out as a triangle, associated with harmony, and described as 'the *tetraktys* which contains the fount and roots of eternal nature'.[43] Who might she have been, this fourfold source of life?

A similar figure was described by Timaeus in his account of the creation. The world we see was made as a copy of the Living Creature, he explained, which God had created as a model:

> The Living Creature embraces and contains within itself all the intelligible Living Creatures ... a Living Creature, one and visible, containing within itself all living creatures which are by nature akin to itself.

> The model is an eternal Living Creature, and [the Father] set about making this universe ... of a like kind.[44]

There were as many forms of life as there were in the Living Creature: gods, winged creatures of the air, creatures of the water, and those that walk on dry land.[45] These corresponded to the elements fire, air, water and earth respectively. The gods, visible as stars, were made mostly of fire, and had only two ways of moving: rotating and going straight forward – rather like the Living One that Ezekiel saw. The other three classes of creatures were created by the angels and not by the Creator, who could only create gods like himself. Genesis, we recall, says nothing of the creation of angels, but does attribute

---

[42] W. Burkert, *Lore and Science in Ancient Pythagoreanism*, tr. E. L. Minar, Cambridge, MA, Harvard University Press, 1972, pp. 468, 165.

[43] This is found in many texts, e.g. Aetius 1.3.8.

[44] Plato, *Timaeus* 30CD, 37D.

[45] Plato, *Timaeus* 40A.

the creation of the material world to *'elohim*, a word that could mean angels.

The Pythagoreans venerated the *tetraktys*, 'the fount and roots of eternal nature'; Timaeus described the Living Creature in whom was all life. Unless the Pythagoreans had two sources of life in their system, which is unlikely, the Living Creature Timaeus described must have been fourfold, which makes Ezekiel's Living One a likely antecedent.

A similar fourfold figure appears in many gnostic texts, Barbelo, a name known only in its Greek and Coptic forms but most likely derived from a Semitic original such as *bᵉ'arba' 'eloah*, the fourfold female divinity. The fullest picture of Barbelo is in the *Secret Book of John*, a Nag Hammadi text. Irenaeus, writing about 185 CE, knew the contexts of this book, and so it represents a relatively early example of Jesus teaching the mysteries to his disciple John. Barbelo, we learn, was the first to come forth from the Father, his image reflecting his light, and she was the womb of everything. Barbelo was the Mother-Father and the eternal aeon among the invisible ones.[46] Barbelo was 'the aeon endowed with the patterns and forms of those who truly exist, the image of the hidden one ...'[47] A hymn addresses Barbelo:

> We bless you for you have unified the entirety from out of the all. You stood at rest, you stood at rest in the beginning, you have become divided everywhere, you have remained one.
> We bless you, producer [fem.] of perfection, aeon giver [fem.] ... and thou art one [fem.] of the one [masc.].
> We have beheld that which is really first existent ... For your light is shining on us ...[48]

She was also the mother of Sabaoth, one of the many names for Yahweh in these texts.[49]

Much of what is said about Barbelo is drawn from the Wisdom texts of the Old Testament, and so those who described her must have thought she was Wisdom. We cannot know if the other things said about Barbelo were additions to the Wisdom figure, or if they were part of the original picture that just did not survive in the

---

[46] *Secret Book of John*, CG II.1.4–5.
[47] *Allogenes*, CG XI.3.51.
[48] *The Three Steles of Seth*, CG VII.5.121–5.
[49] Thus Epiphanius, *Panarion* 25.2.

biblical texts. The 'womb of everything' is like our proposed reading of Ezekiel's vision; and the source of the 'Forms' and patterns was the throne, as we shall see. Other characteristics are clearly paralleled in the Wisdom texts of the Old Testament. For example, Barbelo as 'the first to come forth from the Father, his image reflecting his light', is like 'she was brought forth ... the first of his works' (Prov. 8.22, 25, my translation) and 'she is a reflection of eternal light ... an image of [God's] goodness.'[50] Barbelo addressed as 'you have become divided everywhere, you have remained one' is like 'Though she is but one, she can do all things, and while remaining in herself, she renews all things.'[51] Those who venerated Barbelo knew her as Wisdom, and had their cultural roots in temple tradition.

The throne as the Mother of the LORD appears in Christian culture from east to west; it was not an isolated local phenomenon, which suggests it was known from the beginning and spread with the faith.

- Jacob of Serug, a Syrian writing in the early sixth century CE, composed a homily on 'the chariot that Ezekiel saw', and revealed that he was steeped in temple mysticism. He wrote of the mystery, of God the hidden One, of the angels as sons of light. He prayed for a new mouth to sing the heavenly song, and he knew that the human form on the throne was the Son. The throne itself was Mary: 'The throne and seat upon the chariot ... an image of the Virgin Mother ...'[52] Now Jacob may well have been in touch with contemporary Jewish mystics, but the source of his imagery is not their *merkavah* texts but the older temple mysticism, and he is further proof that this passed into the Church.
- The great Byzantine Akathistos hymn to Mary depicts her as Ezekiel's chariot throne and uses other images from the temple tradition. Nobody knows when the hymn was composed, but Jacob could have known it. She is hailed as 'a throne for the king'; as 'the all-holy chariot of him who rides upon the cherubim'; as 'the vessel of the Wisdom of God, the storehouse of his providence'; as 'the bridal chamber of a marriage without seed'; and as 'the greater holy of holies'.

---

[50] Wisdom of Solomon 7.26.
[51] Wisdom of Solomon 7.27.
[52] A. Golitsin, 'The Image and Glory of God in Jacob of Serug's Homily', *St Vladimir's Theological Quarterly* 47 (2003), pp. 323–64.

- In the western Church the Lady *is* the throne of Wisdom, not, as is sometimes implied, seated on the throne of wisdom. She is most familiar, perhaps, on the seal of Walsingham, which shows her in the style of the *sedes sapientiae*, the seat of Wisdom with her Son enthroned; and in the Litany of Loreto, where she is hailed as the seat of Wisdom.

The throne in the temple had been formed from *cherubim*, the name which Philo said meant 'full knowledge and much science', representing 'knowledge poured out in abundance'.[53] There is nothing in the Hebrew word to suggest this meaning, but the association of the throne, the Lady and Wisdom shows why Philo could think in this way. Wisdom's child was born when he was enthroned, and when he was anointed, the gifts of Wisdom were poured out on him. Dionysius, whose writings are full of allusions to temple mysticism, related the mystery of baptism to this temple rite: '[The anointing oil] gives sweet odour to the one who has been initiated, for the perfect divine birth joins the initiates together with the Spirit of the Deity.'[54]

The Forms

When Ezekiel received his vision of the chariot throne and described what he saw, he used two words that must have been technical terms: *dᵉmut* and *mar'eh*. Most English versions obscure the pattern, but the AV translates these words consistently: *dᵉmut* as 'likeness' and *mar'eh* as 'appearance'. In biblical Hebrew the word *dᵉmut* is used for a comparison ('*as* of a great multitude', Isa. 13.4) and its related verb means to plan ('as I have *planned*, so shall it be', Isa. 14.24), so the overall meaning is not so much a likeness as a thought or a concept preceding an action. The word *mar'eh* means both appearance and a supernatural vision. Reading Ezekiel's description of the chariot throne with these definitions in mind, he is describing something that has emerged from the invisibility of the holy of holies. Dionysius, referring to Ezekiel's visions, taught that this was only a way of trying to express what was beyond words:

---

[53] See above, p. 98.
[54] Dionysius, *The Ecclesiastical Hierarchy* 404C, in *Pseudo-Dionysius. The Complete Works*, tr. C. Luibheid, New York: Paulist Press, 1987.

We cannot, as mad people do, profanely visualize these heavenly and god-like intelligences as actually having numerous feet and faces ... The Word of God makes use of poetic imagery when discussing these formless intelligences, but ... it does so not for the sake of art, but as ... as a concession to the nature of our own mind.[55]

Ezekiel received his visions in the summer of 593 BCE, and it is important to bear in mind the relative dates of the material we are about to compare. Plato, who died in 348 BCE, recorded the teachings of his master Socrates, who died in 399 BCE. Timaeus, as we have seen, was a Pythagorean, and Pythagoras is said to have spent time in 'Syria' in the mid-sixth century BCE, that is, shortly after Ezekiel received his visions.

In the *Timaeus*, as well as in several other dialogues, Plato attributes to Socrates and to Timaeus the theory of Forms which, given that Plato wrote in Greek and Ezekiel in Hebrew, are very similar to Ezekiel's technical terms. Non-material Forms are, they said, the only true reality, and every object or quality in the material world is a copy of the eternal Form which is, in effect, its essence. The Forms exist beyond space and time, and there is a curious description in the *Phaedrus* of this state on the outer surface of heaven which is beyond words: 'the colourless, formless, and intangible truly existing essence with which all true knowledge is concerned holds this region, and is visible only to the mind ...'[56] Timaeus summarized a long exposition by saying:

If this is so, it must be agreed that there exist, first, the unchanging Form, uncreated and indestructible, admitting no modification and entering no combination, imperceptible to sight or the other senses, the object of thought; second, that which bears the same name as the Form and resembles it, but is sensible, has come into existence, is in constant motion, comes into existence in and vanishes from a particular place, and is apprehended by opinion with the aid of sensation; third, space which is eternal and indestructible, which provides a position for everything that comes to be ...[57]

[55] Dionysius, *The Celestial Hierarchy* 137AB, in *Pseudo-Dionysius. The Complete Works*, tr. C. Luibheid, New York: Paulist Press, 1987.

[56] Plato, *Phaedrus* 247c.

[57] Plato, *Timaeus* 52a.

When God was creating the world, he said, the elements were all without 'proportion or measure' and so 'His first step, when he set about reducing them to order was to give them a definite pattern of shape and number . . .'[58]

The state where the Platonic Forms exist sounds very like the holy of holies: beyond space and time, the state of true knowledge, and on the outer surface of heaven, which would correspond to the state beyond the veil of the temple. The mystery of the holy of holies was not accessible to ordinary human senses, just as the state of the Forms was visible only to the mind. Ezekiel's system is like the Forms, and the priestly tradition which shaped his thought is evidence of 'Forms' some two centuries before Socrates. Pythagoras could have learned about them when he was in 'Syria', and his disciple Timaeus expounded them in his dialogue with Socrates.

These are Ezekiel's likeness-appearance passages, quoted from the AV:

- 'Out of the midst [of the fire] came the likeness of four living creatures. And this was their appearance; they had the likeness of a man [or possibly, as in 1.10, and 10.16, they had one likeness]' (Ezek. 1.5).
- 'As for the likeness of the living creatures, their appearance was like burning coals of fire, and like the appearance of lamps . . .' (Ezek. 1.13).
- 'The appearance of the wheels and their work was like unto the colour of a beryl: and they four had one likeness; and their appearance and their work was as it were a wheel in the middle of a wheel' (Ezek. 1.16).
- '. . . over their heads was the likeness of a throne, as the appearance of a sapphire stone: and upon the likeness of the throne was the likeness as the appearance of a man above upon it' (Ezek. 1.26).
- 'As the appearance of the [rainbow], so was the appearance of the brightness round about. This was the appearance of the likeness of the glory of the LORD' (Ezek. 1.28).
- '. . . a likeness as the appearance of fire: from the appearance of his loins even downward, fire; and from his loins even upward, as the appearance of brightness, as the colour of amber' (Ezek. 8.2).

---

[58] Plato, *Timaeus* 53b.

- 'There appeared over [the cherubims] as it were a sapphire stone, as the appearance of the likeness of a throne' (Ezek. 10.1).
- 'And the likeness of their faces was the same faces which I saw by the river of Chebar, their appearances and themselves: they went every one straight forward' (Ezek. 10.22).

If Ezekiel understood $d^e mut$ to be the invisible reality in the holy of holies, and *mar'eh* its appearance in his vision, his description is consistent. The invisible reality of the four living creatures appeared to him in human form (Ezek. 1.5), like fire (Ezek. 1.13). Enoch recorded the same phenomenon: on his first heavenly journey, he saw 'those who were like flaming fire, and when they wished they appeared as men'.[59] Ezekiel also saw that the $d^e mut$ of the throne appeared to him as a sapphire stone (Ezek. 1.26; 10.1), and the $d^e mut$ of the glory of the LORD *appeared* like a bright rainbow surrounding a fiery human figure. The heavenly reality presumably could manifest itself in various ways, and in Ezekiel's vision it was as a fiery human being. Enoch saw holy sons of God walking on flames of fire[60] and Ezekiel described a guardian *cherub* who was driven out from the midst of the stones (sons?) of fire (Ezek. 28.16).[61] Enoch also saw the fallen angels whose spirits, 'assuming many different forms, defile mankind'.[62]

The *mar'eh* of the $d^e mut$ of the LORD may well account for the mysterious 'Word', *logos*, of the LORD, which Philo used in the sense of 'God made visible', and so 'word' in our sense is not the best translation. Philo said, for example, that the elders who ascended Sinai with Moses '*saw* the Logos'.[63] It is widely agreed that underlying Philo's Logos was the Aramaic phrase in the Targums, 'the *memra* of the LORD', usually translated 'the Word of the LORD', but could the older belief in the visionary appearance, *mar'eh*, of the LORD be the origin of 'the memra of the LORD'? Scholars admit that the meaning of *memra* is no longer known: 'At some point in the tradition, the content of *memra* was lost; how or why we do not clearly know.'[64] It

---

[59] *1 Enoch* 17.1.

[60] *1 Enoch* 71.1.

[61] See below, pp. 136–7.

[62] *1 Enoch* 19.1.

[63] Philo, *Confusion of Tongues* 96.

[64] C. T. R. Hayward, 'The Memra of YHWH and the Development of its Use in Targum Neofiti', *Journal of Jewish Studies* XXV (1974), pp. 412–18, p. 418.

may have been because 'seeing the LORD' was controversial, and texts which suggested this were read differently. The vision of the LORD became the Word of the LORD.

The *dᵉmut* could appear in a vision as *mar'eh*, but also as a physical reality. The earliest instance of this is in the Genesis creation story, where Adam is 'as our image, *tselem*, according to our *dᵉmut*' (Gen. 1.26, translating literally). Adam was the physical reality, not a vision. When the actual male and female were created as physical realities (Gen. 1.27), the *dᵉmut* is not mentioned, since the male and female distinction is a physical phenomenon, *tselem*, and not present in the *dᵉmut* of God. The account of the birth of Seth should be read in the same way: he was the *dᵉmut* of Adam and his physical image. Both these texts are from a priestly writer, a near contemporary of Ezekiel and presumably using the same terminology.[65] The *dᵉmut* of the divine was not always manifested in human form: in the temple there was bread of the presence, which 'was' the divine presence and imparted this to the priests who ate it: 'their most holy food' (Lev. 24.5–9, my translation). This was the divine in physical, but not human, form. Dionysius knew that the divine could be present in both the bread and the human: '[The bishop] uncovers the veiled gifts . . . He shows how Christ emerged from the hiddenness of his divinity to take on human form.'[66]

The early Christians knew of the hidden 'Forms' in the holy of holies, and their temple heritage means this was not borrowed from Platonism. There are few examples of early hymns, and temple themes predominate: the enthronement, as we have seen, and the pairing of 'Form' and manifestation: 'Christ Jesus . . . in the form of God . . . born in the likeness of men . . .' (Phil. 2.5–7); and 'He is the image of the invisible God' (Col. 1.15). There were also enigmatic early texts such as the *Gospel of Philip*, but in this context, their meaning is clear. The Christians prayed to be united to the angel images, presumably to their own *dᵉmut*, and thus become what God intended them to be: 'He said on that day, in the Thanksgiving, *eucharistia*, "You who

---

[65] Another near-contemporary was the Second-Isaiah, who used these technical terms to mock those who made idols. 'To whom will you *dᵉmut* God? And what is the *dᵉmut* you will set out for him?' (Isa. 40.18, translating literally). The best the idol maker can do is make an image, *pesel*, that cannot even move.

[66] Dionysius, *Ecclesiastical Hierarchy* 444C.

have joined the perfect, the light, with the Holy Spirit, unite the angels with us also, the images ..."'; and 'If you become light, it is the light which will share with you. If you become one of those who belong above, it is those who belong above who will rest in you.' And there are passages like this one, where the bridal chamber is the the place of the 'Forms' by which the creation is ordered:

> At the present time we have the manifest things of creation ... Contrast the manifest things of truth: they are weak and despised, while the hidden things are strong and held in high regard. The mysteries of truth are revealed though in type and image. The bridal chamber, however, remains hidden. It is the holy in the holy. The veil at first concealed how God controlled the creation ...[67]

The *d^emut* and its physical realization may be how Psalm 110.4 was understood: 'You are a priest for ever, *after the order of* Melchizedek' was an important Christian proof text. The original Hebrew words *'al dibrāthi* do not have this meaning elsewhere, and the Syriac translation[68] chose *badmutah*, saying that the king was the *d^emut* of Melchizedek. This explains Hebrews 7.15: 'another priest arises in the *likeness* of Melchizedek', and suggests that Melchi-Zedek was a heavenly 'Form' with several physical manifestations. Theodotus, the second-century Egyptian Gnostic, whose ideas were very similar to those in the *Gospel of Philip*, said something similar: the Son was 'drawn in outline in the Beginning'.[69]

The Qumran *Songs of the Sabbath Sacrifice* show more of the fiery world of the holy of holies, and introduce more technical terms, but the texts are fragmented and damaged. Each *d^emut* was engraved within the holy of holies. 'The wondrous *d^emut* of most holy spirit engraved ... the [*d^em*]*ut* of living *'elohim* engraved in the vestibule where the King enters, figures of spirits of light ...'[70] Another term, which had a similar meaning to *d^emut*, was *tsūr* (pl. *tsūrot*): 'spirits of the knowledge of truth and righteousness, in the holy of holies, *tsūrot* of living *'elohim*, *tsūrot* of luminous spirits, figures of the *tsūrot*

---

[67] *Gospel of Philip* CG II.3.58, 79, 84.

[68] Known as the Peshitta, the 'simple' version. The Old Testament was translated from the Hebrew in perhaps the second century CE.

[69] Clement of Alexandria, *Excerpts from Theodotus* 19.

[70] *Sabbath Songs*, 4Q405.14–15.

of *'elohim* engraved round about . . .'[71] In later Jewish texts, the *tsūrot* were angels, but in the Hebrew scriptures *tsūr* has often been obscured because the same letters can mean 'rock'. In each of the following examples, the word 'rock' does not appear in the Lxx, which suggests that the translator did not think the text was about a rock. The lines make good sense if *tsūr* is translated 'Invisible One': 'The God of Israel has spoken, the *Rock* of Israel has said to me . . .' (2 Sam. 23.3): 'The *Rock*, his work is perfect; for all his ways are justice . . .' (Deut. 32.4); 'He forsook the God who made him, he scoffed at the *Rock* of his salvation . . .' (Deut. 32.15); 'Is there a God, *'eloah*, besides me? There is no *Rock*. I know no other' (Isa. 44.8, my translation).[72]

In the *Songs of the Sabbath Sacrifice*, the *tsūrot* in the holy of holies were 'engraved', presumably their way of describing a distinct entity in a state without time or matter. Another hymn declares: 'Everything is engraved before you, an inscribed record of the perpetual seasons, and the record of the cycles of the eternal years and their sacred seasons.'[73] There are many of these 'engraved things' in the Hebrew scriptures and they include not only objects but also the laws for human behaviour, just as the Platonic Forms included both objects and qualities. The English translations use a variety of words, and so obscure the pattern, but with a literal translation, it is clear that the engravings preceded the physical creation and so must have existed in the pre-physical state of the holy of holies. Ezekiel's contemporary Jeremiah knew that the pattern of creation had been engraved beforehand: the limits of the sea were fixed by 'an engraving of eternity' (Jer. 5.22, my translation); 'the engravings of the moon and stars . . . if these engraved things should depart from my presence, says the LORD . . .' only then would Israel cease to be (Jer. 31.35–36, my translation). Proverbs cannot be dated with certainty, but the chapter about Wisdom in creation shows she was there when the engravings were made before the creation of the material world. Translating literally: 'When he prepared the heavens, I was there, when he engraved a circle on the face of the deep . . . when he set down for the sea its engraved mark . . . when he engraved the foundations of the earth . . .' (Prov. 8.27–29, my translation). Human life was engraved: 'You have

---

[71] 4Q405.19.

[72] There are many examples.

[73] *Thanksgiving Hymns*, 1QH IX.25b–26.

made his engraving and he cannot pass it' (Job 14.5, my translation; cf. 23.14). All the laws for human life were engraved: the law of Moses was 'engraved things', often translated 'statutes': e.g. Lev. 10.11; Num. 30.16; Deut. 4.6; Ps. 119.5.

In later texts, the engravings were on the throne itself. When the angels were summoned to see Jacob sleeping at Bethel, the LORD said: 'Come, see Jacob the pious whose image is on the throne of Glory.'[74] In *3 Enoch* we see the role of the engravings in the process of creation. R. Ishmael, the high priest, ascended to heaven and was shown the mysteries by Metatron, the great angel who had formerly been Enoch. First he was shown the angels round the throne, who were the morning stars singing and the sons of God shouting for joy (Job 38.7). This was the first stage of creation. Then, as the angels sang the Sanctus, all the holy names engraved on the throne flew off and became the heavenly host, and some went out from under the throne. In other words, as the great angels sang 'Holy, holy, holy is the LORD of Hosts; the whole earth is full of his glory' (Isa. 6.3), the names on the throne became the angels who filled the creation with glory. Then R. Ishmael saw 'the letters engraved with a pen of flame on the throne of glory', the letters by which heaven and earth were created.[75]

This is the scene in Revelation 4—5, where the heavenly beings sing hymns to the One on the throne. The key to understanding this vision is the unusual form of the divine Name.

> Holy Holy Holy is the LORD God Almighty,
> *Who was and is and is to come* . . .
> *For thou didst create all things*
> *And by thy will they existed and were created.*
> (Rev. 4.8, 11, my translation)

The form is like that in the Targums. When the LORD revealed his name at the burning bush, the original text is: 'God said to Moses "I AM WHO I AM"' (Exod. 3.14), but nobody is sure how to translate the Hebrew here: *'ehyeh 'asher 'ehyeh*. The Name elsewhere is *Yahweh*, a third person form. At the burning bush there is the unique first person form, the personal revelation of the Name by its bearer. The Targum implies that the Name did not mean I AM, but rather

---

[74] Targum *Pseudo-Jonathan* Gen. 28.12. This also appears in *Genesis Rabbah* LXVIII.12.
[75] Summarizing *3 Enoch* 38—41.

I WHO CAUSE TO BE.[76] 'He who said to the world from the beginning "Be there" and it was, and is to say to it "Be there" and it will be there.'[77] Targum style required both occurrences of 'I AM' in Exodus 3.14 to be represented, and so the first referred to creation in the past and the second to the future. Thus the form of the Name in John's vision was appropriate in a hymn to the Creator.

> *Who was and is and is to come . . .*
> *For thou didst create all things*
> *And by thy will they existed and were created.*
>
> (Rev. 4.8, 11)

The LORD enthroned at the heart of creation was named as the one who causes to be. Isaiah saw the King, the LORD of Hosts, and if LORD meant 'he who causes to be', then LORD of Hosts meant 'he who causes the hosts to be'.[78] John may have known that the hosts originated as engravings on the throne and became separate beings as they heard the Sanctus.

Genesis 1 alludes to this meaning of the Name. The creation comes into being by the command of *'elohim*: 'Let there be . . .', *y^{e}hiy*, which is from the same verb as 'Yahweh', and the account of the six days of creation ends: 'The heavens and the earth were finished and all their host' (Gen. 2.1, my translation). The 'host' here meant everything in heaven and earth, rather than just 'the heavenly beings', which is why the Lxx has 'the heaven and the earth and all their *kosmos*, order'. Now Pythagoras was the first Greek to use the name *kosmos* for the universe,[79] and one wonders why, especially as the Pythagoreans, with their symbolic names for numbers, said that 6 was *kosmos*.[80]

Two passages in the Qumran *Community Rule* also imply that Yahweh meant 'the One who causes to be'. One of the LORD's ancient titles was the 'God of knowledge' (1 Sam. 2.3), and part of the instruction for the 'sons of light' builds on this title and on the meaning of the Name:

---

[76] The Hebrew verb as a *hiph'il*, causative, form rather than a simple *qal*.

[77] Thus the Fragment Targum of Exodus 3.14. Neofiti and *Pseudo-Jonathan* are similar.

[78] Some of what follows is from W. H. Brownlee, 'The Ineffable Name of God', *Bulletin of the American Schools of Oriental Research*, 226 (1977), pp. 39–46.

[79] Aetius 2.1.1, in G. S. Kirk and J. E. Raven, *The Presocratic Philosophers*, Cambridge: Cambridge University Press, 1957, p. 229.

[80] Iamblichus, *Theologoumena Arithmeticae* 37, ed. V. de Falco, Leipzig: Teubneri, 1922.

From the God of knowledge comes *all that is and shall be. Before ever they existed*, He established their whole design, and when, as ordained for them, *they came into being*, it is in accord with his glorious design that they accomplish their task without change. The laws of all things are in his hand and he provides them with all their needs ...

> *All things come to pass* by his knowledge;
> He establishes all things by his design
> And without him nothing is done.[81]

The God of knowledge brings things into being, which is the *raz nihyeh*, the mystery of becoming. The word *nihyeh* is also from the same root as *Yahweh*. 'Ordained before they came into being' refers to the 'spirits of creatures in heaven and earth' that Moses had seen in Day One, along with the other angels.[82] The singer of the second passage from the *Community Rule* had just sung of marvellous mysteries, of gazing on eternal wisdom concealed from other men, and of the chosen assembly that has joined with the Sons of Heaven.

According to the *Songs of the Sabbath Sacrifice* too, the 'Forms' were engraved, and according to *3 Enoch*, the engraved things became angels. Philo explained how the angels related to the 'Forms', and he was quite clear that what others called Forms, his people called angels. When Moses asked the LORD to show him his glory, wrote Philo, and had explained that 'by thy glory I understand the powers that keep guard around thee', the LORD replied:

The powers that you seek to know are discerned not by sight but by mind ... But while in their essence they are beyond your apprehension, they nevertheless present to your sight a sort of impress and copy of their actual working ... Such you must conceive my powers to be, supplying quality and shape to things which lack either and yet changing or lessening nothing of their eternal nature. Some among you call them not inaptly 'forms' or 'ideas' since they bring form into everything that is, giving order to the disordered, limit to the unlimited, bounds to the unbounded, shape to the shapeless and in general changing the worse into something better.[83]

---

[81] *Community Rule*, 1QS III 15–17; XI.11.
[82] *Jubilees* 2.2.
[83] Philo, *Special Laws* I.47–8.

For temple tradition, then, it was the angels who shaped the visible creation, and the mystics who stood by the throne learned about the creation as they learned about the angels.

The knowledge

Enoch stood by the throne and then recorded what he saw. He called this a vision of Wisdom, and we have it as three parables, not parables like those of Jesus but parables in the sense of visions, which is the other meaning of the word. The *Parables of Enoch*,[84] one section of *1 Enoch*, describe what happened in the holy of holies. They are the most detailed source of information about the 'knowledge' of the temple mystics, the 'secret things' forbidden by the Deuteronomists. The Deuteronomists contrasted the Law, which was also revealed, with the things in heaven (Deut. 29.29; 30.11–14).[85] The text of the *Parables* is disordered in places, there are obvious insertions of related material that break the original sequence, and no part of this section has been found at Qumran. Nevertheless, there is only one context in which these texts make any sense: temple mysticism. The substance of the *Parables* is as old as any Enoch material, even if their present form cannot be dated with certainty. There are several other texts such as *2 Enoch*, *3 Enoch* and the *Merkavah Rabbah*[86] which present the same ideas as the *Parables* but in more detail. What we cannot know is whether the extra detail was known to the author of the *Parables*, or whether it was a later development, albeit within the same cultural tradition. At the very least, the other texts are evidence of how the *Parables* were understood.

In his vision, Enoch stood by the throne, heard the Sanctus, and felt himself transformed. He saw and heard the 'multitude beyond number' and the four presences.[87] Then 'the angel of peace' showed him all the hidden things.[88] This angel appears several times in Enoch's *Parables* as the revealer of the secret things about the creation and about the future punishment of the wicked,[89] but the angels of peace

---

[84] Enoch's parables are sometimes called *The Similitudes of Enoch*.
[85] See above, p. 47.
[86] Meaning 'the Great Chariot Throne'.
[87] See above, p. 67.
[88] *1 Enoch* 40.2.
[89] *1 Enoch* 52.5; 53.4; 54.4.

first appear in Isaiah: 'The angels of peace weep bitterly ... the covenant is broken ... the land mourns and languishes ...' (Isa. 33.7, 8, 9, translating literally). Elsewhere Isaiah shows that this covenant was the eternal covenant, also known as the covenant of peace.[90] Now 'peace', *shalōm*, means more than 'peace' in our sense of the word; it means complete, perfect – everything that the creation was intended to be – and when the covenant was broken, the creation began to collapse. The same letters also mean 'retribution', *shillem*, and so the angel of peace in Enoch's vision also presided over punishment. The angel of peace was the angel of the covenant of peace, and when he showed Enoch the knowledge of the creation, and how the kingdom was divided and yet bound together, he was in fact revealing himself. The pairing of peace and punishment was known to the early Church: John saw the kingdom of the Messiah proclaimed on earth with reward for the servants and punishment for the destroyers (Rev. 11.18). The text of Revelation is Greek, but beneath was the old temple wordplay: *shalōm* and *shillem*, but also serve = *'ābad*, and destroy = *'ibbad*.

After he had been transformed, Enoch saw 'all the secrets of heaven and how the kingdom is divided, and how the actions of men are weighed in a balance'. This is a summary of what follows in the *Parables*.[91] The kingdom, as we have seen, was the holy of holies, and so Enoch learned how the original Unity was divided into the many of the visible creation, and then how sinners would be punished. First he saw the secrets of the thunder, lightning and winds; then he saw the secrets of the sun, moon and stars, and how they were bound to their orbits by a great oath, and how the LORD of Spirits called them all by name. Three key words appear for the first time: the lightnings and stars were '*weighed* in a *righteous* balance, according to their *proportions* of light'. The basis of the covenant of peace, i.e. the order of creation, was the great oath, which included correct weights, measures and proportions, and 'righteousness', which meant everything in its assigned place.[92]

In his second *Parable*, Enoch saw the Chosen One in human form, enthroned in glory. This Man 'had' righteousness, in other words, he

---

[90] Isaiah 24.4–6 uses the same vocabulary.

[91] *1 Enoch* 41.1. D. W. Suter, *Tradition and Composition in the Parables of Enoch*, Missoula: Scholars Press, 1979, pp. 40–141, first suggested this.

[92] *1 Enoch* 41, 43, 44.

had the power to restore and uphold righteousness, and so too the power to judge the unrighteous. Enoch saw the heavenly reality that was replicated on the day of atonement in the temple – the offering of the life/blood of the Righteous One to restore the broken everlasting covenant – and then he saw by the throne the fountain of righteousness and the fountains of wisdom. Since Wisdom was the perception to keep everything in right order, righteousness and Wisdom here are synonymous. The Chosen One was then named, i.e. given the Name. Since the vision was set in the holy of holies, the Chosen One was given the Name 'before the sun and the signs were created, before the stars of heaven were made'.[93] Then all on earth worshipped him – a now-familiar scene. The Chosen One sat in judgement, and all the metals of the earth melted like wax at his feet and so lost their power: no more iron or bronze or tin to make weapons, no more lead, no more silver or gold.[94]

This was proof of triumph over the fallen angels, who had rebelled, broken the original harmony and corrupted the earth with their knowledge. The earliest material in *1 Enoch* says that Azazel, the leader of the fallen angels, had begun the corruption of the earth by teaching men about metal working: how to make weapons and jewellery which led to war and fornication.[95] Isaiah knew this too: his oracles – and so, we assume, the religion of the first temple – show no knowledge of the Ten Commandments, but they do condemn a land filled with silver, gold and war chariots, and women decked in jewellery (Isa. 2.6–8; 4.18–23). Azazel appears once in the Hebrew scriptures (Lev. 16.7–10), represented by the scapegoat who was ritually banished and imprisoned each year on the day of atonement when the blood of the Righteous One was taken into heaven.[96] Scholars are puzzled about this ritual with Azazel – further evidence, were it needed, that temple tradition has been neglected.

In his third *Parable*, Enoch saw future blessings for the chosen and righteous ones in the light of eternal life. There follows a longer account of the hidden things and their divisions and measurements – how the winds are weighed, how the stars are divided – and then a

---

[93] *1 Enoch* 48.3.

[94] *1 Enoch* 52.1–9.

[95] *1 Enoch* 8.1–2.

[96] They understood Leviticus 16.8 to mean that the goat was 'as Azazel', not 'for Azazel'.

description of the angels responsible for the various natural phenomena: angels of hoar frost and hail, angels who lead out the spirit of the rain and so on.[97] These angels are also described in *Jubilees*: 'the angels of the spirit of fire ... of the winds ... of the clouds and darkness and snow and hail and frost ... of thunder and lightning ... of cold and heat and winter and springtime and harvest and summer ...'[98] In the third *Parable* there is another account of the fallen angels and their teachings which destroyed the creation, and how they tried in vain to learn from the archangel Michael the hidden Name in the oath that secured the created order. Fragments of a poem survive here, describing how the great oath secured the heavens and the earth, the limits of the sea, the orbits of the sun, moon and stars.[99] These were the bonds of the eternal covenant, that Isaiah knew had been broken when the creation began to wither away, and which caused the angels of peace to weep. The bonds were restored on the day of atonement, when the high priest sprinkled the life/blood, put the sins of Israel onto the scapegoat and then called out the Name, the audible sealing of the renewed creation.[100] This is the likely context for the penitential *Prayer of Manasseh*[101] which addressed the LORD like this:

> Thou who hast made heaven and earth with all their order;
> Who hast shackled the sea with thy word of command,
>   who confined the deep
> And sealed with thy terrible and glorious Name ...
>
> (*Prayer*, 3)

The Enochic picture of creation secured by the bonds of the covenant and sealed with the Name was the world view of the first temple. Isaiah described the broken bonds of creation, and Ezekiel described the seal. The text is difficult to read, because we do not really know what it is about, but Ezekiel described an anointed *cherub* who was 'the seal of proportion, *toknit*' or 'the seal of the pattern, *tabnit*',[102]

---

[97] *1 Enoch* 58, 60.

[98] *Jubilees* 2.2.

[99] *1 Enoch* 69.

[100] Mishnah *Yoma* 6.2.

[101] A text from the late second temple period that was included in a collection of Odes appended to the Psalter in the fifth-century Codex Alexandrinus.

[102] Both words look similar in Hebrew.

created full of wisdom and dressed like a high priest. The *cherub* was thrown from heaven because s/he[103] abused wisdom and became unrighteous (Ezek. 28.12–19), in other words, failed to uphold the covenant which must have been the role of an anointed *cherub* high priest. Now the high priest wore the Name on his forehead on a golden seal, but the prescription for this in Exodus should be read 'Engrave on it the engravings of a holy seal belonging to the LORD' (Exod. 28.36, my translation). In other words, the seal bore just the Name, and since at least the time of Ezekiel, the Name was represented by a diagonal cross.[104]

Yet again, this is found in the *Timaeus*, and Justin, writing in the mid-second century CE, knew that Plato had taken this from 'Moses'. Justin had studied philosophy before he became a Christian and he was certain that not only the bonds but also the X-shaped seal described by Plato had originated in the Hebrew scriptures. Plato wrote:

> [God] then took the whole fabric and cut it down the middle into two strips, which he placed crosswise at their middle points to form a shape like the letter X; he then bent the ends round in a circle and fastened them to each other opposite the point where the strips crossed.[105]

Plato described these bonds as the soul, which both enveloped the world and was woven right through it, 'the soul invisible and endowed with reason and harmony'.[106] We recognize this soul as 'Wisdom' who held all things together in harmony (Lxx Prov. 8.30), and 'pervades and penetrates all things' (Wisd. 7.24).

The other Enoch texts give more detail: *2 Enoch* says he was anointed and transformed into an angel and then instructed in all the things of heaven and earth.[107] Finally, he taught his children: 'Now therefore, my children, I know everything; some from the lips of the LORD, others my eyes have seen from the beginning [of creation] even to

---

[103] This is another passage with a mixture of masculine and feminine forms, like Ezekiel's visions of the chariot throne.

[104] The angels were told to put a 'mark' on the faithful, literally a letter *tau*, which at that time was written X (Ezek. 9.4–6).

[105] Plato, *Timaeus* 36, and Justin, *Apology* I.60.

[106] Plato, *Timaeus* 37.

[107] *2 Enoch* 22.8—23.4.

the end.'[108] He then gave lists of measurements and numbers in the creation. Teaching such as this must have been known to the early Christians. What else might John have had in mind when he wrote 'You have been anointed by the Holy One and you know all things' and 'His anointing teaches you about everything' (1 John 2.20, 27)?

In *3 Enoch*, there is much more about the names and roles of the angels that were mentioned briefly in the second *Parable*, and, as we have seen, about the names engraved on the throne. It is clear that the angels 'were' the natural phenomena, and so learning about the angels was learning about the creation. Angel lore was the natural science of the time, and they were the invisible principles that modern science would call 'the laws of nature'.[109] Dionysius, as we have seen, expressed the same idea:

> Through [the angels'] mediating efforts, he who is the Cause and indeed the author of all purification has brought out from the domain of the hidden, the workings of his own providence down to the point where they are visible to us.[110]

The earliest known list of angel names was found at Qumran in a fragment of Enochic text. They are all formed from *'el*, God, and the name of some natural phenomenon: *Ramt'el*, meaning burning heat of God; *Kokab'el*, meaning star of God; *Ra'm'el*, meaning thunder of God; *Matar'el*, meaning rain of God, and so on.[111]

A similar text to *3 Enoch* is the *Merkavah Rabbah*[112] and although it shows temple tradition being later adapted for magic – 'using the mystery' – it still preserves valuable older material. Central to the great mystery was the *Shema'*, the affirmation that the LORD our *'elohim* is One. Once he had learned this mystery of the unity, the mystic could see the world in a new way:

---

[108] *2 Enoch* 40.1.

[109] The difference between angels and laws of nature is that angels are living beings and so can effect changes in creation which the laws of nature can only describe.

[110] Dionysius, *Celestial Hierarchy* 308A.

[111] Reconstructed by J. T. Milik, in *The Books of Enoch. Aramaic Fragments of Cave 4*, Oxford: Clarendon Press, 1976, p. 152. The names are the earlier forms of those in *1 Enoch* 8.3.

[112] As with all these texts, the precise date of composition is unknown, but the material has consistent and recognizable traits.

Ishma'el/he said: When my ears heard this great mystery,
The world was changed around me into a shining place
and my heart was as if I/it had come to a new world,
and every day it seemed to my soul
as though I was standing before the throne of glory.[113]

In the *Merkavah Rabbah*, the mystery was sometimes called the *middoth*, literally 'the measurements', because measurement and proportion were all part of the engraved system. The *cherub* high priest was the seal of the proportion/plan, and the *Gospel of Philip* said that Messiah meant both anointed and measured (or perhaps measurer?).[114] A Jewish text from the early second century CE says Moses was taught the measurements when he was on Sinai: the measures of fire, the depths of the abyss, the weight of the winds, the number of the raindrops, the height of the air . . . He also saw the root of wisdom and the fountain of knowledge, the angels, archangels and so on.[115]

The measurements in the engraved plan were known to Ezekiel, but he expressed it differently. The temple represented the creation, and so the measurements of the temple symbolized right order in the natural world and in human society. A fiery 'man' with a measuring reed appeared to Ezekiel and told him the correct measurements for the new temple (Ezek. 40.1–4). Ezekiel had to tell this to his people: 'Describe the temple to the house of Israel that they may be ashamed of their deviations/iniquities and measure the plan/ proportion' (Ezek. 43.10, translating literally). 'Deviate', '*āwāh*, meant both to twist and to sin, and so the prophet concluded his list of temple measurements by condemning the princes of Israel and exhorting them to justice and righteousness, putting things right. These included honest weights and measures in the market place (Ezek. 45.9–12)!

***

Temple mystics saw the throne and learned the secrets of the holy of holies. The Qumran texts tell of the *raz nihyeh*, the mystery of how things come into being, or, in the words of *1 Enoch*, how the

---

[113] *Merkavah Rabbah* 680.
[114] *Gospel of Philip*, CG II.3.62.
[115] *2 Baruch* 59.5–12.

kingdom is divided.[116] Temple mystics knew that engravings from the throne emerged to shape the material world. They also knew that the obedience of the angels, which they described as their worship and their music, held the many in unity. The priestly service in the temple and the music of the Levites replicated the heavenly reality, not as 'creation' but as re-creation, that is, as atonement.

Ezekiel saw the throne, and upon it, the *d^emut* of the glory of the LORD which appeared in his vision as a fiery Adam. The LORD – 'he who causes to be', the Creator – was seen as a human form. The story was that Adam had lost the vision and no longer knew the *d^emut*: 'Because of sin, it was not given to man to know the *d^emut* on high; were it not for this, all the keys would be given to him, and he would know how the heavens and the earth were created.'[117] When Adam lost the vision, he also lost Wisdom, the knowledge that enabled him to uphold the covenant and thus to preserve the creation. The Qumran community hoped to regain Adam's former and intended state and they described themselves as people whom 'God has chosen for an everlasting covenant'. They hoped to regain 'all the glory of Adam' and so to learn 'the knowledge of the Most High . . . the Wisdom of the sons of heaven'.[118] We now look at the human figure who was to re-occupy the throne, who regained the lost glory, the heavenly knowledge and the angelic wisdom, and who restored the everlasting covenant. He was called the Servant.

---

[116] *1 Enoch* 41.1.

[117] Attributed to R. Nathan, who lived in the mid second century CE, in *Abot de R. Nathan* 39.

[118] *Community Rule*, 1QS IV.

5

The Servant

The Servants of the LORD were the temple mystics. In the Hebrew scriptures the word servant usually meant a slave or a subject, but there are places where 'Servant' seems to be a title with special significance. A servant could be a worshipper. 'Service' was an act of worship, and 'serving the service' was the technical term for the work of the Levites: 'minister at the tabernacle' (Num. 3.8) is literally 'to serve the service of the tabernacle'. The levitical singers were servants of the LORD in the temple (Pss 134.1; 135.1), and the prophets were also servants of the LORD (Jer. 7.25; Ezek. 38.17; Amos 3.7; Zech. 1.6). Great men were called servants: 'My servant Abraham' (Gen. 26.24); 'My servant Moses' (Num. 12.7; Mal. 4.4), 'My servant David' (Ps. 89.20; Ezek. 34.23, 24). All these men had seen the LORD: Abraham saw the LORD at Mamre (Gen. 18.1); Moses spoke with the LORD face to face and saw his form, $t^e munah$ (Num. 12.7–8); David saw the Man ascending (1 Chron. 17.17, if that is the meaning of this opaque text). 'My servant the Branch', on the other hand, was a messianic figure (Zech. 3.8); and the Servant of the LORD described by Isaiah (e.g. Isa. 42.1; 52.13) was the Messiah according to the Targum and the early Christians, but not according to the MT.[1] The Servant attracted the attention of the correcting scribes.

'Servant' was the preferred title for Jesus in the early Jerusalem Church: Peter spoke of God's Servant, *pais*, Jesus, who was also the Holy and Righteous One, the Author of Life and the Messiah (Acts 3.13–18). The Jerusalem Christians recognized that Jesus 'thy holy Servant', *pais*, had been anointed and had fulfilled Psalm 2 – 'the LORD and his anointed' – and that signs and wonders had happened 'through the name of thy holy servant, *pais*, Jesus' (Acts 4.27, 30). An early hymn extolled Christ Jesus who had taken the form of a servant, *doulos*, when he became incarnate (Phil. 2.7). The earliest known

---

[1] See below, p. 156.

account of the Eucharist outside the New Testament is in the *Didache*, which uses 'thy Servant Jesus': the prayer over the bread was 'We give thanks to thee, our Father, for the life and knowledge thou hast made known to us through thy Servant Jesus'; and the thanksgiving after receiving the wine and bread was: 'Thanks be to thee, holy Father, for thy sacred Name which thou hast caused to dwell in our hearts, and for the knowledge and faith and immortality which thou hast revealed to us through thy Servant Jesus . . .' 'To us thou hast graciously given spiritual meat and drink, together with life eternal, through thy Servant . . .'[2]

The Greek words used for 'Servant' in these examples were all translations from the underlying Hebrew or Aramaic, and so *pais* and *doulos* simply show different translators. The word *pais* can also mean a child, which explains 'thy holy Child Jesus' in some English versions. The least obvious of the translations was John's 'Lamb of God', a title that involves not only wordplay but also the old temple code of describing humans as animals and heavenly beings as 'men'. The wordplay is that the Aramaic for servant was *talyā'*, literally a young one, and this could also mean a lamb. The Lamb in the book of Revelation was the Servant in his heavenly aspect, and the temple code using 'animals' and 'men' means that the Lamb enthroned in heaven was the human figure whom Isaiah and Ezekiel had seen enthroned. A lamb with seven eyes and seven horns is a creature from science fiction and a warning against reading Revelation too literally. What John saw was the Lamb/Servant, enthroned, filled with the sevenfold light and the sevenfold Spirit, standing, that is, resurrected, even though it had been killed (Rev. 5.6–7).

Men and angels

The 'animals and men' code is important for understanding a core belief of the temple mystics which can be demonstrated from *1 Enoch*. One section of it, the *Dream Visions*, tells the Enochic version of the history of Israel and Jerusalem. The good human characters are all ritually clean animals, and the enemies are all unclean animals. Thus Adam was a white bull and the 12 sons of Jacob were white sheep,

---

[2] *Didache* 9, 10.

whereas the Egyptians were wolves[3] and the offspring of the fallen angels and their human wives were elephants, camels and asses.[4] The biblical story is that the offspring were the fallen ones, *nephilim*, and the mighty men, *gibborim* (Gen. 6.4). The Enochic version is fuller and says the offspring were giants and *nephilim*, but also *elioud*, possibly a corruption of Hebrew *yeled* = child.[5] These names show the sophistication of the wordplay in the animal histories: elephants, camels and asses are all Aramaic puns and anagrams on the names *nephilim*, *gibborim* and *elioud*.[6] Thus it is no coincidence that the Servant in his human state was called the Lamb; the name was the same.

Angels were 'men'. Enoch was taken up to a lofty place by three 'men' in white[7] and a 'man' recorded all the sins of the shepherd angels who had been unfaithful.[8] This is found in the Bible too: the man Gabriel came to Daniel (Dan. 9.21); an angel measured the heavenly city 'by a man's measure, that is, an angel's' (Rev. 21.17); and on Easter morning, the women at the tomb saw two men in shining clothes, whom they said were angels (Luke 24.4, 23). Since 'son of man' means just a human being,[9] *'Son of Man' used as a title meant the Man, a heavenly being in human form.* Daniel saw one 'like a son of man'[10] coming with clouds (Dan. 7.13), in this instance, the human going to be enthroned and thus transformed into a divine being. For John, this was the Lamb approaching the throne (Rev. 5.1–14). Jesus told a parable about sheep and goats, i.e. human beings, when the Son of Man came with his angels for the judgement (Matt. 25.31–46). Some 'animals' became 'men', which was the Enochic code for *theosis*: Noah was born a bull and became a man, Moses was a sheep who became a man.[11]

The *Gospel of Philip* shows the difference between 'animals' and 'men', and so implies what happened at the transformation. A broken text has been reconstructed: 'There are two trees growing in Paradise.

---

[3] *1 Enoch* 85.3; 89.12, 14.

[4] *1 Enoch* 86.4.

[5] *1 Enoch* 7.2.

[6] Suggested by J. T. Milik, *The Books of Enoch. Aramaic Fragments of Qumran Cave 4*, Oxford: Clarendon Press, 1976, p. 240.

[7] *1 Enoch* 87.2–3.

[8] *1 Enoch* 90.14, 17.

[9] There has been huge controversy over this expression when used of Jesus.

[10] 'Like' here is just the preposition, not the word 'likeness'.

[11] *1 Enoch* 89.1, 36.

The one bears [? animals] the other bears men. Adam [? ate] from the tree that bears animals and he became an animal ... [? If he] ate the [ ] fruit of the [. . .] bears men . . .'[12] The gist is clear; eating from the forbidden tree made Adam an animal, but had he eaten from the tree of life, he would have been a man. The text is then even more broken, but seems to say that had Adam remained in his intended state, the 'gods' would worship him.[13] The difference between an animal and a man was Wisdom, because '[Wisdom] is a tree of life to those who lay hold of her . . .' (Prov. 3.18). Jesus promised his faithful followers that they would again be able to eat from the tree of life (Rev. 2.7; 22.14), that is, be restored to Adam's intended state as a 'man'.

In order to set the (Son of) Man into his context, we need to look briefly at what the first Christians could have known about Adam, which is far more than the Genesis story. Adam lost his status as the 'Man', and the Servant regained it. Jesus was called the Servant but also the second Adam (1 Cor. 15.45–50), the one who reversed Adam's loss of Eden.

First, there is Ezekiel's version of the Adam and Eden story: he described a jewelled anointed *cherub* who was thrown from Eden (Ezek. 28.12–19). This *cherub* was dressed as a high priest, according to the Lxx, but the MT lists fewer jewels (Ezek. 28.13) and has lost the link to the high priest. The *cherub* was created as the seal of the plan/the proportion, presumably the one who sealed the eternal covenant; he was full of wisdom and perfect in beauty (Ezek. 28.12), walking among the stones/sons of fire. Due to the pride, corruption, iniquity and unrighteousness that made his sanctuaries unholy places, the *cherub* was thrown to earth and became mortal. This is a more exotic figure than the Genesis Adam, but may well have been how Ezekiel knew him. Like the Genesis figure who is initially male-and-female, the *cherub* was described with a mixture of masculine and feminine forms, and there is a strong suspicion that he was not originally the king of Tyre. 'Tyre', *tsōr*, is written in the same way as *tsūr*, the engraved archetype in the holy of holies,[14] and the almost opaque verse that describes the high priest's jewels also mentions what may be 'engravings' – but this word is not known for certain elsewhere.

---

[12] *Gospel of Philip*, CG II.3, 71.
[13] This is a reference to the non-biblical story of Adam enthroned. See below.
[14] See above, p. 120.

We can never know exactly what Ezekiel wrote, but the translator of the Lxx thought that the wise *cherub* thrown from Eden was a high priest, and the Qumran *Songs of the Sabbath Sacrifice* described the angel priests as jewelled 'engravings'. Perhaps the anointed wise *cherub* was originally the heavenly archetype of the high priest.

Jewish tradition did remember Adam as the original high priest. Comparing the six original stages of assembling the tabernacle and the six days of creation[15] shows that the purification of the high priests corresponded to the creation of Adam (Exod. 40.30–32; Gen. 1.26–31). The text of Genesis also implies that Adam was the high priest in Eden. The familiar words that he was set in the garden 'to till it and keep it' (Gen. 2.15) are both technical temple terms: 'till', *'ābad*, meant to perform temple service, to be the Servant; and 'keep', *shāmar*, meant to preserve the tradition/teaching. No ancient discussion considered Adam as a gardener; he was the high priest.[16] He wore garments of glory, and an older version of Genesis said God had made for the human pair garments of light, *'ōr*, rather than garments of skin, *'ōr*.[17] Ben Sira described Wisdom as a garment of glory (Ben Sira 6.30–31), and another Jewish text, the *Apocalypse of Moses*, said Adam had worn a garment of glory and righteousness.[18] Christians knew this too: Ephrem, writing in fourth-century Syria, said that God had clothed Adam with glory,[19] and a Wisdom text from Nag Hammadi had Wisdom speaking to her children: 'I am giving you a high priestly garment woven from every wisdom ... clothe yourself with wisdom like a robe ... be seated on a throne of perception ... return to your divine nature.'[20] This garment is not mentioned in Genesis, but it is assumed: when the human pair listened to the snake and were tempted by his wisdom and the chance to be like the *'elohim*, 'they knew they were naked' (Gen. 3.7).

Another story was that when Adam was created as the image of the LORD, Michael commanded all the angels to worship him. Satan

---

[15] See above, p. 14.
[16] *Genesis Rabbah* XVI.5.
[17] The high priest's vestments were for glory and beauty (Exod. 28.2). They were called 'garments of light' in R. Meir's scroll, see *Genesis Rabbah* XX.12, the scroll taken as loot from the temple in 70 CE.
[18] *Apocalypse of Moses* 20.1–2.
[19] Ephrem, *Commentary on Genesis* 2.
[20] *The Teaching of Silvanus*, CG VII.4.89, 91.

refused, saying that he had been created before Adam, and so Adam should worship him. Satan was then thrown from heaven and vowed the revenge on Adam described in Genesis.[21] Although this story is not in the Bible, it is the background to Psalm 2: the LORD set his king in Zion, called him his son, and then commanded the kings and rulers to worship him (Ps. 2.12). The king in Zion was Adam, the image of the LORD enthroned there, and what Ezekiel saw, 'the appearance of the likeness of the glory of the LORD', was 'the likeness of the appearance of Adam', enthroned (Ezek. 1.28, 26 AV). Adam was high priest and king. This story was the context for Jesus' temptations in the wilderness; the devil wanted the second Adam to worship him (Luke 4.5–7), to reverse his ancient humiliation, but Jesus refused and was enthroned 'with the wild beasts, and the angels served him' (Mark 1.13, my translation). This was also the context of Deuteronomy 32.43, quoted as a proof text in Hebrews: 'When he brings the first-born into the world, he says, "Let all God's angels worship him."' 'First-born' was a royal title ('I will make him the first-born . . .' Ps. 89.27), and also Adamic; it was used of Jesus in an early hymn: 'He is the image of the invisible God, the first-born of all creation . . .' (Col. 1.15).

Adam was commanded to 'be fruitful and multiply, and fill the earth . . .' (Gen. 1.28), but all these words have other meanings: 'be fruitful', *pārāh*, is similar to 'be beautiful/glorified', *pā'ar*, and 'multiply', *rābāh*, can also mean 'be great'. Jewish tradition remembered the other meanings. The original Adam was beautiful and great and filled the earth, and everything he had lost would be restored in the time of the Messiah: 'his lustre, his immortality, his height, the fruit of the earth and the fruit of the trees and the luminaries'.[22] Adam was also commanded to subdue, *kābash*, the earth and have dominion, *rādāh*, over other living creatures (Gen. 1.28). These words, translated this way, have caused great problems: did Adam have a mandate to exploit the earth? Now *kābash* usually means 'subdue' but seems to have another meaning at Micah 7.18–19. The context here is atonement: 'He will again have compassion on us, he will *kābash* our iniquities', and since the image used for atonement was restoring the broken bonds of the covenant, *kābash* here seems to mean' bind up'. Adam

---

[21] *The Life of Adam and Eve* 12—16.
[22] Attributed to a Rabbi of the late third century CE, in *Genesis Rabbah* XII.6.

binding up the earth is consistent with Ezekiel's Adam-*cherub* being the seal, and with other texts, as we shall see. His other role, to have dominion, *rādāh*, was like Solomon's dominion: he ruled, he had dominion, and there was peace all round him (1 Kings 4.21, 24). This understanding of Adam was also used of Jesus; that hymn in Colossians continues: 'He is before all things, and in him all things hold together . . .' (Col. 1.17).

Adam was the Man, the meaning of his name. He was the original high priest, the Son of God (Luke 3.38), the one intended to sit on the throne of the LORD as king, vested in garments of glory and full of wisdom. He was set in Eden as the Servant, a radiant heavenly figure, the seal of the eternal covenant. He had to rule so that there was peace all round, in other words, uphold the covenant in the state that was called 'righteousness'.

With this picture of Adam the Man in mind, we look at the *Parables of Enoch*, which often use the title Son of Man and describe this Man and his relation to Enoch. Enoch's Son of Man looked like an angel, he 'had righteousness', he revealed the hidden things, and he sat in judgement on the kings and the mighty ones.[23] He was the Righteous One whose blood was offered in heaven and who was then given the Name.[24] Some of Enoch's description of the Son of Man suggests he was the unfallen Adam: he was radiant, he had knowledge, he was enthroned. Other details suggest he was Isaiah's Servant: offering his blood, a light to the Gentiles, the 'Chosen One' who had received the Spirit of wisdom, understanding, insight and might.[25] The Enochic Son of Man is part-unfallen Adam and part-Servant, suggesting that unfallen Adam and the Servant were two elements of the same figure. The Son of Man was also Enoch. In one of the most unexpected and thus most debated sections of the *Parables*, 'Enoch' described his own transformation into the heavenly Son of Man, his own *theosis*.[26]

Similar material is found in *2 Enoch*, where Enoch stood before the throne, and the LORD instructed Michael: 'Take Enoch from his earthly clothing, and anoint him with my oil of delight and clothe him with the clothes of my glory.' These were the garments of light

---

[23] *1 Enoch* 46.1–8.
[24] *1 Enoch* 47.1—48.2.
[25] *1 Enoch* 49.2, suggesting that Enoch knew the Servant as the Messiah of Isaiah 9.
[26] *1 Enoch* 70.1–2; 71.14.

(Ps. 104) that Adam had worn. When Enoch had been anointed with a sweet shining oil, like dew perfumed with myrrh, and then vested with garments of glory, he knew he had become one of 'the glorious ones'.[27] Enoch had returned to the state of the unfallen Adam, with his radiant face and garment of glory and wisdom.

In *3 Enoch*, his transformation is assumed: R. Ishmael the high priest[28] was guided round heaven by the great angel who had formerly been Enoch.[29] His angel name was Metatron, and he was enthroned in heaven. Like Adam, all the angels had to worship him.[30] Metatron was frequently called 'youth', *na'ar*, which also meant 'servant'.[31] Many meanings have been proposed for the name/title Metatron. Eusebius drew on many Old Testament texts – Psalm 110 and especially Psalm 45 – and then wrote of the Messiah: 'This is he who is called the beloved of the Father and his offspring and the eternal priest and the *being called the sharer of the Father's throne*.'[32]

Such *theosis* was known to the early Christians. These are two examples of several in the *Odes of Solomon*, thought to be early Christian baptismal hymns, but the imagery was from the royal birth rites in the holy of holies.

> He lightened my eyes and my face received the dew;
> and my nostrils/my breathing enjoyed the pleasant
> odour of the Lord . . .[33]

> She brought me forth before the face of the Lord,
> And although I was a son of man,
> I was named the illuminated one, the son of God
> while I praised among the praising ones,
> and great was I among the mighty ones.
> For according to the greatness of the Most High, she[34]
> made me;

---

[27] *2 Enoch* 22.8–10.

[28] *3 Enoch* 1.1; 2.3. Several other texts, e.g. Babylonian Talmud *Hullin* 49a, say that R. Ishmael was a priest.

[29] *3 Enoch* 4.1–3.

[30] *3 Enoch* 10, 14.

[31] *3 Enoch* 2.2; 3.2; 4.1, 10.

[32] Eusebius, *Proof of the Gospel* IV.15.

[33] *Odes of Solomon* 11.14–15, in J. H. Bernard, *The Odes of Solomon*, Cambridge: Cambridge University Press, 1912.

[34] 'Spirit' is a feminine noun in Syriac.

and according to his own newness he has renewed me;
and he anointed me from his own perfection
And I became like one of his neighbours.[35]

Since the perfumed anointing oil was an imitation of the true oil of Wisdom that was extracted from the tree of life, temple anointing conferred a different way of knowing. There is ample evidence for this in early Christian writings.[36] In the *Clementine Recognitions*, Peter explained to Clement:

> Although indeed he was the Son of God, and the beginning of all things, he became man. God first anointed him with oil taken from the wood of the tree of life: from that anointing he is called Christ. He . . . anoints with similar oil all the pious when they come to his Kingdom . . . so that their light may shine, and being filled with the Holy Spirit, they may be endowed with immortality . . .
>
> In the present life, Aaron the first high priest was anointed with a composition of chrism, an imitation of the spiritual ointment . . . If then this temporal grace, compounded by men, was so effective, how potent was that ointment extracted by God from a branch of the tree of life.[37]

Wisdom as the oil is mentioned in Ben Sira, but not explained. Wisdom served in the temple – implying she was a priest or high priest – and she 'was' the perfumed oil:

> Like cassia and camel's thorn I gave forth the aroma of spices,
> And like choice myrrh I spread a pleasant odour,
> Like galbanum, onycha, and stacte . . .   (Ben Sira 24.15)

These were the ingredients of the holy oil, made to imitate what Moses had been shown on Sinai (Exod. 30.22–25; cf. Exod. 25.9). Dionysius was preserving ancient temple tradition when he wrote a whole chapter about the meaning of the perfumed oil in his *Ecclesiastical Hierarchy*: 'It spreads its sweet fragrance into their mental reception . . . the transcendent fragrance of the divine Jesus distributes its conceptual gifts over our own intellectual powers.'[38] He

---

[35] *Odes of Solomon* 36.3–6.

[36] See my book *The Great High Priest*, London: T&T Clark, 2003, pp. 129–36.

[37] *Clementine Recognitions* I.45–6.

[38] Dionysius, *The Ecclesiastical Hierarchy* 476B, 477C, in *Pseudo-Dionysius. The Complete Works*, tr. C. Luibheid, New York: Paulist Press, 1987.

knew it was the sacrament of divine birth: 'In being initiated in that sacred sacrament of the divine birth, the perfecting anointing of the ointment gives us a visitation of the holy Spirit.'[39]

There were many titles for the one who had been anointed with the holy oil and transformed into a 'Man', but not all were in use at the same time. Metatron, for example, is likely to be a later title for the (Son of) Man. In the New Testament the Servant was also the Holy and Righteous One, the Author of Life and the Messiah; the one who fulfilled Psalm 2; the one whose Name wrought miracles; the one who poured out his life and was then exalted; the one given the Name and the sealed scroll, and then worshipped by all creation. Most of these indicate that he had a key role in temple mysticism, and the others – pouring out his life, the Righteous One – indicate the context for the main celebration of mystical belief. It was the day of atonement.

Before looking at the original meaning of this rite, we must return to Enoch himself, and to his experience of transformation. At the end of the third *Parable*, Enoch was identified as the Son of Man. Scholars long resisted this translation, presumably because they did not wish to find what it said, but recently discovered early manuscripts of *1 Enoch* confirm that Enoch was indeed identified as the Son of Man.[40] He was swept up to heaven, saw the mighty angels and the throne, and was then declared to be the Man. He was 'born to righteousness', perhaps meaning 'born as the Righteous One', to bring peace from the world to come. He would have 'length of days' and the righteous would never leave him.[41] This must have been the role of Melchi-Zedek, king of Salem, of whom an early Christian could write in Hebrews: 'He is first, by translation of his name, king of righteousness, and then he is also king of Salem, that is, king of peace' (Heb. 7.2). Over-literalism has obscured many connections, as has the fragmentation that came from assuming that one figure could not have many titles.[42]

The New Testament evidence alone shows that Jesus the Son of Man was the Servant, the Holy and Righteous One, the Author of Life

---

[39] Dionysius, *Ecclesiastical Hierarchy* 484C.
[40] See D. Olson, *Enoch. A New Translation*, North Richland Hills: Bibal Press, 2004, p. 134.
[41] *1 Enoch* 71.1–17.
[42] The evil angel in the Qumran *Testament of Amram* 4Q544 has three names.

and the Messiah (Acts 3.13–18); he was the anointed one of Psalm 2 (Acts 4.27); he had emptied himself, died and then been exalted to receive the worship of all creation (Phil. 2.7–11); and, according to John, had been baptized with the Spirit as Son of God, and so was the Messiah, the King of Israel and the Lamb who takes away the sin of the world (John 1.32–51). In the *Didache* the Servant had made known life and knowledge, faith and immortality. Messiah, Son of God and King of Israel show that the Servant was a royal figure; the Holy One could mean an angel; the Righteous One means the one who makes right, the one who restores the covenant; the Author of Life suggests temple mysticism, as do the life, knowledge and faith of the *Didache*. Exaltation to the throne in heaven after death and resurrection (or after emptying himself), suggest that the Servant figure originated in the older temple cult, before the changes wrought by the Deuteronomists, and that the Christians – and doubtless others too – remembered who he was. The context for renewing the creation covenant and then enthroning the Messiah was the sequence of temple festivals in the autumn, the new year in the old calendar. Of these, the day of atonement is the most difficult to reconstruct.

The day of atonement

The ritual for the day of atonement is described in Leviticus 16, a complicated text with several insertions and repetitions such that the original is beyond reconstruction. It sets out what the high priest had to do on the day of atonement, the one day in the year when he was allowed to enter the holy of holies. Two goats were chosen by lot: one was sacrificed and its blood used in the ritual; the other – the 'scapegoat' – was loaded with the sins of Israel and driven out into the desert. The high priest entered the holy of holies of the tabernacle/temple and sprinkled blood/life on the mercy seat/throne. He acted alone. Then he returned to the outer part of the tabernacle/temple and sprinkled the blood/life in various places to cleanse and consecrate the temple/creation. Finally, he drove the sin-bearing goat into the desert (Lev. 16.1–22).

It used to be the fashion in Christian Old Testament scholarship to say that the day of atonement was a late addition to Israel's temple cult, a sign of unfortunate foreign influences in the second temple period.[43] This was a problem for Christians, for whom atonement is central to their understanding of the role of Jesus, and led to Christian teachers stating with some confidence that the idea of cosmic atonement must have seeped into Christianity from pagan systems.[44] Jewish scholars thought differently: the old *Jewish Encyclopedia* said the day of atonement was 'the keystone of the sacrificial system of post-exilic Judaism',[45] and now, largely due to the work of Jacob Milgrom,[46] the ritual is thought to be very old indeed. Some non-Jewish scholars had earlier suspected this. W. R. Smith wrote in the 1920s: 'The worship of the second temple was an antiquarian resuscitation of forms which had lost their intimate connection with national life and therefore had lost the greater part of their original significance.'[47] It seems that the ritual for the day of atonement was ancient and the key temple rite, even though its original significance had been partly lost in the second temple. Add to this the facts that Deuteronomy omitted the day of atonement from its calendar (Deut. 16) and that someone of a similar mind denied that one person could make atonement for another (Exod. 32.30–34), and we have a context for the original day of atonement and a reason for the loss of its original meaning. It was part of the royal cult which assumed the older story of the creation; and it was lost after the purges in the time of Josiah.

There is more detail in the *Mishnah* about the day of atonement ritual at the end of the second temple period, but, as happens with the *Mishnah*, there is no theology. Nothing explains why certain things were done, but it does show how the detail in Leviticus was understood. The high priest was prepared with ritual immersions at daybreak, and then dressed in his golden vestments for the morning sacrifices and burning the incense. This is not mentioned in Leviticus. Then he was immersed again and dressed in white linen to enter the holy of holies (as in Lev. 16.4). The two goats for the ritual had to

---

[43] E.g. T. K. Cheyne, *Jewish Religious Life after the Exile*, New York: Putnam, 1898, pp. 75–6.
[44] Famously F. W. Dillistone, *The Christian Understanding of Atonement*, Philadelphia: Westminster Press, 1968, p. 47.
[45] 'Day of Atonement' in *The Jewish Encyclopedia*, New York: Funk and Wagnalls, 1901–06.
[46] E.g. J. Milgrom, *Leviticus 1–16*, New York: Doubleday, 1991.
[47] W. R. Smith, *Lectures on the Religion of the Semites*, 3rd edn, London: A & C Black, 1927, p. 216.

be identical in every way,[48] a detail not in Leviticus. The high priest had to cast lots and assign each goat its role: one was 'for Azazel' and the other was 'for the LORD' (as in Lev. 16.8). He sacrificed a bull as an offering for himself and his house (as in Lev. 16.11), and put some of its blood in a bowl. Then he took incense into the holy of holies so that the smoke would cover the mercy seat (or, presumably, the throne). This was where the LORD appeared, 'in the cloud upon the mercy seat' (Lev. 16.2). The *Mishnah* says the incense had to be set where the ark had formerly been.

Next he took the bull's blood into the holy of holies and sprinkled it seven times before the mercy seat and on the mercy seat. When he emerged, he put the bowl of blood on a stand in the temple, a detail not in Leviticus.[49] Then he sacrificed the goat 'for the LORD', took its blood into the holy of holies and sprinkled it in the same way. When he emerged, he sprinkled the veil with each blood separately, before pouring the remainder of the bull's blood into the goat's blood, and then poured the mixed bloods back into the original bowl.[50] These details of sprinkling the veil and how the bloods were mixed are not in Leviticus. He took the mixed bloods and sprinkled the golden altar in the temple and the great altar outside, before pouring the remaining blood at the base of the outdoor altar so that it could drain away underneath.

Finally, the high priest put both his hands onto the head of the live goat and transferred to it all the sins of Israel. These the goat took away with him into the desert. According to the *Mishnah*, the high priest at this moment called out the Name, not using some reverent substitute such as Adonai, but actually pronouncing the Name.

What did all this mean? There are only a few clues in Leviticus: first, that blood was life (Lev. 17.11), and that blood 'atoned', that is cleansed and restored, the holy place and the tent of meeting. The blood purified from all the effects of the people's sin, but only the priests could enter the holy places, and so the holy places had not literally been polluted by the presence of sinners. From other sources we conclude that, since the tabernacle/temple represented heaven and earth, the high priest was taking blood into heaven and

---

[48] Mishnah *Yoma* 6.1.
[49] Mishnah *Yoma* 5.3.
[50] Mishnah *Yoma* 5.5.

then returning to earth to remove from the earth the effect of human sins. This was the renewal of the creation at the new year. Isaiah described the destruction of the creation as breaking the bonds of the eternal covenant (Isa. 24.4–5), and the day of atonement ritualized life from heaven restoring the broken bonds of the eternal covenant. The song of the Levites – perhaps the renewing song – was part of the process.[51]

Restoring the covenant by atonement was the duty of the high priest, whose very presence repaired the breach and thus secured the created order when it was threatened with wrath. Two examples show how this process was imagined: after the rebellion of Korah, wrath broke out in the form of plague, and many died. Aaron had to take his incense, the sign of priesthood, and make atonement: 'He made atonement for the people. And he stood between the dead and the living; and the plague was stopped' (Num. 16.47–48). The story was later retold with more detail: Aaron intervened and overcame the wrath because he wore the divine majesty on his diadem – the Name – and his ministry showed that he was the servant of the Lord (Wisd. 18.20–24). In other words, the high priest showed he was the Servant of the Lord by restoring the covenant with his presence. Aaron's grandson Phineas, also a high priest, turned back the wrath when an Israelite man had broken covenant law, and thus put his whole people in danger. Phineas killed him and his forbidden wife, and from this point he was given the 'covenant of peace . . . because he . . . made atonement for the people of Israel' (Num. 25.10–13). Atonement involved both repairing the broken covenant bond and also dealing with the sin that had caused the breach. These were the two roles of the angel of peace: *shalōm*, peace, and *shillem*, punishment.

There is an ancient hymn appended to Deuteronomy that describes the Lord coming to judge sinners and to atone the land of his people (Deut. 32.43), and this is what the high priest was doing. He 'was' the Lord, and he wore the Name. The verse, however, received the attention of the correcting scribes. The MT is no longer clear, and the older version found at Qumran and represented in the Lxx is twice the length of the post-Christian MT. This, then, is another question: why should a text about the Lord coming to bring judgement and

---

[51] See above, p. 87.

to atone the land have been a 'sensitive' matter? The reason is that this verse, in its original longer form, was a proof text used of Jesus by the early Church; he was the LORD, the great high priest, coming to judge and atone, and one of the lines missing from the MT, 'Let all God's angels worship him', is quoted at Hebrews 1.6.

The high priest and the blood of the goat must together have represented the LORD coming to heal the land and his people. The high priest, as we have seen, represented the LORD, and so too did one of the goats. One was 'for Azazel', apparently, and one was 'for the LORD'. Now a goat sacrificed to the LORD is no problem, but a goat for Azazel, the leader of the fallen angels, is a considerable problem. Origen provides the answer. When he moved from Alexandria, he settled in Caesarea which was a considerable centre of Jewish learning, and he had contact with Jewish scholars. He said that the goat sent out into the desert was not *for* Azazel, but 'as Azazel'.[52] The Hebrew preposition *l^e* can mean both 'for' and 'as', and so *la$^{'a}$zā'zēl* could mean 'as Azazel', just as Solomon was anointed 'as king', *l^{e}melek* (1 Kings 1.34, my translation). If one goat represented Azazel, the other goat represented the LORD. The blood/life of the sacrificed goat represented the 'life' of the LORD, and this was used to cleanse and renew the creation. Since the high priest also represented the LORD, he was in effect renewing the creation with his own life/blood. Thus the writer of Hebrews explained: 'But when Christ appeared as a high priest . . . he entered once for all into the Holy Place, taking not the blood of goats and calves but *his own blood*, thus securing an eternal redemption' (Heb. 9.11–12).

Hence the titles in Peter's temple sermon, which happened sometime after Pentecost, and the theme suggests it was delivered around the day of atonement: 'Repent . . . that your sins may be blotted out . . .' (Acts 3.19). He named Jesus as the Servant who had been glorified, the Holy and Righteous One, the Author of Life. All these titles are appropriate to the high priest on the day of atonement: righteousness was the state of the restored covenant, as we shall see,[53] and so the Righteous One would have effected this; and the Author of Life was the LORD who gave his life/blood to renew the creation. Peter

---

[52] Origen, *Against Celsus* 6.43. The Greek and Latin versions of the text are both clear on this point.

[53] See below, p. 165.

continued with day of atonement imagery: 'that times of refreshing may come from the presence of the LORD' (which meant the high priest bringing the new life out from the holy of holies); 'that he may send the Christ appointed for you' (which meant that the high priest returning from the holy of holies led to the hope for the second coming).

The meaning of the blood mingling has been lost. The logic, if there can be such an approach to ritual, is that the mortal life of the human high priest, represented by the bull's blood, was mingled with the heavenly life of the LORD, represented by the goat's blood, and that the two together were sprinkled in the outer part of the temple to repair the covenant bonds and renew the creation. *This is exactly how the creation was described by Timaeus*, presumably recounting the teaching of Pythagoras. 'Between the being which is indivisible and remains always the same and the being which is transient and divisible into bodies, he mixed in the middle a third form of being . . .' When they had been mixed to form the soul, the Creator distributed them in accordance with the intervals of the musical scale, and also – the text is not clear – cut the whole into two strips which he formed into two circles, one within the other, that were joined with an X. The material world was formed within this structure, but the soul also permeated it, 'woven right through from the centre to the outermost heaven'. This sounds rather like the 'wheel within a wheel' (Ezek. 1.16) around the Living One. The soul was 'invisible and endowed with reason and harmony'.[54] The whole rather confused account sounds like the temple ritual of (re)creation: the divine life (the goat's blood) was mixed with the human life (the bull's blood), and the mixture was distributed so as to create/restore the harmony of creation. Pythagoras's/Timaeus's account of the creation, had it come from the first temple, would have known the role of Wisdom, and so their 'soul' had that role, holding all things together in harmony (cf. Lxx Prov. 8.30), and permeating the whole creation (cf. Wisd. 7.27; 8.1). The similarity is striking. Now these latter – the Lxx of Proverbs and the Wisdom of Solomon – could have been written with *Timaeus* in mind, but if so, the question becomes: Why did the writers of Lxx Proverbs and the Wisdom of

---

[54] Plato, *Timaeus* 35–7.

Solomon describe Wisdom and the bonds of creation as the world soul of Timaeus?

The high priest transferred the sins of Israel onto the head of the second goat, which implies, if there was any 'logic' to the ritual, that the high priest was carrying the sins at the time. By sprinkling his 'own' blood, he absorbed into himself the effect of the sin and renewed the covenant bonds. This idea is set out in Leviticus: Moses was angry with two high priests because they had burned the sin offering and not eaten it. They should have eaten the offering so as to 'carry', *nāśā'*, the iniquity of the people. This verb means both to carry and to forgive: those who carried iniquity forgave it. The priests carried sin and so did the Lord, but the same verb is usually translated 'forgive' when the Lord is the subject: 'Who is a God like you, bearing/ forgiving sin? (Mic. 7.18). Wearing the Name protected the high priest in his dangerous role: it enabled Aaron to 'bear, *nāśā'*, the guilt', the uncleanness, in any of the offerings that were brought (Exod. 28.38, translating literally). So too the commandment, originally to the high priest: 'You shall not bear, *nāśā'*, the Name lightly, for the Lord will not consider free from guilt the one who takes/wears his Name lightly' (Exod. 20.7, translating literally). The high priest, wearing the Name and sprinkling the blood/life of the Lord, was able to restore the covenant bonds. When this was done, he called out the Name, which was the seal of the bonds.

Leviticus and the *Mishnah* show how the atonement ritual was performed, and we have reconstructed something of the meaning, but so far without a context. There are several other texts where one or other part of the atonement ritual is described or assumed, and conflating these may give something of the original theological and liturgical setting. The problem with using other texts like this is: did the writers of these texts know an extended ritual context from which they drew what they needed; or did these writers construct their texts from a variety of *previously unconnected* older materials? The latter is usually assumed but the assumption is not acknowledged; I shall assume the former. I also assume that this was a living tradition with established forms of expression, and that later texts were not simply compiled from earlier written sources, in the manner of some modern research.

Twice in the New Testament there is 'pouring out' of blood: the 'Servant' emptied himself and was then given the Name and exalted to receive the homage of all creation (Phil. 2.6–11). The early Church knew that the blood ritual preceded enthronement, and the hymn implied a known connection between the pouring out and the exaltation: '*therefore* God has highly exalted him . . .' (Phil. 2.9). And Matthew's account of the last supper, which had to distinguish between the various covenants in the Hebrew scriptures because it was written for Hebrew Christians, made clear that Jesus renewed the eternal covenant: 'This is my blood of the covenant, which is poured out for many for the putting away of sins' (Matt. 26.28, translating literally).[55] Of the covenants described in the Old Testament, only the one renewed on the day of atonement dealt with the putting away of sins. At the last supper Jesus, the great high priest, inaugurated the great high priestly ritual of atonement by pouring out his own blood.

The hymn in Philippians linked the pouring out of the Servant and his enthronement, and so the 'one like a son of man' whom Daniel saw enthroned was also the Servant, but the blood ritual is obscured in modern translations. The 'one like a son of man' was 'presented' to the Ancient of Days (Dan. 7.13), but the verb here, $q^e r\bar{e}b$, is the technical term for making a temple offering, and so the Man was 'offered' to the Ancient of Days. This was the blood offering. In the Philippians hymn the Servant was given the Name, the moment of *theosis*, and this happened with Daniel's 'Man' but is also lost in translation. Comparing the two Greek translations, we see that the *theosis* disappeared from the post-Christian translation, even though both Greek versions were made by Jews. The older Lxx has 'he came as, *hōs*, the Ancient of Days', in other words, the Man *was* the Ancient of Days, but the post-Christian version by Theodotion has 'he came to, *heōs*, the Ancient of Days'. The post-Christian Jewish translation did not include the *theosis* of the Man, which is the meaning of the enthronement scene in Revelation 5. The Servant/Lamb was sacrificed and resurrected, and then enthroned. At this point, the Lamb and the One on the throne became a single figure, as we have seen,[56] just as Daniel's Man came 'as the Ancient of Days'.

---

[55] There is no 'new' covenant in $\mathfrak{P}^{37}$ and $\mathfrak{P}^{45}$, which are third-century papyri; nor in the Sinai codex and the Vatican codex, which are fourth-century texts. These are the oldest evidence for this part of Matthew.

[56] See above, p. 104.

The fullest account of the day of atonement is in Enoch's second *Parable*, which tells the unseen story: what happened in heaven when the blood was taken into the holy of holies. Enoch saw the Head of Days (Daniel's 'Ancient of Days') and he saw the Son of Man who looked like one of the angels. This Man was the Righteous One who would reveal the hidden things and judge the mighty. The main action happened after the prayers of the righteous ones had reached heaven, together with the blood of the Righteous One.[57] Then the holy ones in heaven offered prayer and praise with one voice, 'on behalf of the blood of the righteous ones', the Son of Man was given the Name, and all on earth worshipped him. This *Parable* links the blood offering in heaven to the *theosis* and enthronement of the Righteous One, in other words, it shows that sprinkling blood on the mercy seat/throne (Lev. 16.15) was the enthronement. As the Man was given the Name, Enoch chose that moment to describe the fountains of righteousness and wisdom where the thirsty could drink.[58]

This *Parable* has imagery from the Davidic kings and from Isaiah's Servant songs. The Enochic Son of Man is the Chosen One who sits on the throne of the LORD of Spirits (i.e. the LORD of Hosts),[59] just as Solomon sat as king on the throne of the LORD (1 Chron. 29.23). Isaiah's Servant was the Chosen One (Isa. 42.1), but Isaiah does not mention any enthronement. Enoch's Son of Man was also the Righteous One whose blood was offered,[60] he was a light to the Gentiles,[61] and he had been hidden: 'From the beginning the Son of Man was hidden . . . and the Most High revealed him to the Chosen . . .'[62] The Servant in Isaiah was described in all these ways, as we shall see, and even though the *Parables of Enoch* do not use the title Servant, the Man figure offering blood and being enthroned in the holy of holies was the Servant. The identity of Enoch's Son of Man was revealed by the angel of peace as one of the 'hidden things',[63] and John the Baptist also saw himself as the revealer. After declaring that Jesus was the Lamb of God, that is, the Servant, who

---

[57] *1 Enoch* 47.1, 4.

[58] *1 Enoch* 48.1–2.

[59] *1 Enoch* 51.3.

[60] Also at *1 Enoch* 53.6, and 38.2, at the opening of the first *Parable*.

[61] *1 Enoch* 48.4–6.

[62] *1 Enoch* 62.7.

[63] *1 Enoch* 46.1–2.

takes away the sin of the world, he said: 'I myself did not know him; but for this I came baptizing with water, that he might be revealed to Israel' (John 1.31).

Finally, there was the atonement that Melchizedek would bring. The Qumran Melchizedek text,[64] though fragmented, applies texts to Melchizedek which in the Hebrew scriptures apply to the LORD or to *'elohim*. We have already seen how correcting scribes obscured the fact that Melchizedek was the LORD,[65] but this Qumran text confirms that he was indeed the LORD. Melchizedek was to return at the beginning of the tenth Jubilee,[66] and the day of atonement at the end of that Jubilee would be the year of Melchizedek's favour (cf. Isa. 61.2, the year of the LORD's favour). Although the text is broken, it is clear that Melchizedek was the one anointed with the Spirit to bring the good tidings (Isa. 61.2–3) to proclaim his kingdom (Isa. 52.7), and to bring the judgement.

From this collection of texts, we could conclude that the Servant was the human being who reversed the fall of Adam. He was the Davidic king, the Chosen One (thus Ps. 89.19), who had been transformed and enthroned as the human image of the LORD, he was the Son, and he was Melchizedek. He was the Righteous One whose blood/life restored the creation. In the autumn festival, the blood offering to heal the creation was made on the day of atonement, and the enthronement of the king was celebrated six days later at Tabernacles.

The Servant in Isaiah

Jesus identified himself as the Servant in Isaiah. He spoke many times of the prophesied suffering and rejection of the son of man, one of the ways he described the Servant (Mark 8.31; 9.12, 31; 10.33). Of these, only 9.12 does not mention the resurrection, suggesting that Jesus understood the exaltation of the Servant as resurrection, that is, he understood it in the temple sense of the word. On the road to Emmaus, so Luke's sources told him, Jesus explained to two disciples

---

[64] 11QMelchizedek.

[65] See above, p. 106.

[66] This was the time of Jesus's baptism; see my book *The Great High Priest*, London: T&T Clark, 2003, pp. 33–41.

that he had fulfilled the prophecy: 'Was it not necessary that the Anointed One should suffer these things and enter into his glory?' (Luke 24.26, my translation). There is no such prophecy in the MT, but there is in the Qumran text of Isaiah 53, which has some significant differences from the MT. This text attracted the attention of the correcting scribes. Since there are several ancient sources to help in the reconstruction of the original text and its meaning – the Qumran scroll and the MT, but also the Lxx, parts of the post-Christian Greek translations, and the Targum – this investigation will need to be more detailed than any other in this book, *because of the importance of the text for establishing the antiquity of temple mysticism, and also for illuminating how Jesus was understood by his first followers.* What follows is not an exhaustive study of the fourth Servant song, but only of the main points immediately relevant to temple mysticism and the early Christian use of this text.

There are four passages in Isaiah, usually called the *Servant Songs* (Isa. 42.1–4; 49.1–6; 50.4–9; 52.13—53.12), that were first grouped together by Bernhard Duhm in his 1892 commentary. The *Servant Songs* is not an ancient designation, but this group of texts does describe a striking figure whom the Christians recognized as prophetic of Jesus. Scholars do not agree as to the origin of the 'songs': some say they were a much later addition to the Isaiah scroll; others that they were prophecies from the First-Isaiah, re-used by a disciple writing perhaps 150 years later, in the turmoil of the mid-sixth century BCE and possibly in exile in Babylon. They were given a new context, where the Servant represented the whole people suffering in exile: 'Israel my Servant, ... I have chosen you and not cast you off ...' (Isa. 41.8–9). Nor is there agreement as to the extent of the Servant material; the second and third songs may include additional lines at the end, or these may be later comment on them.

The fourth song (Isa. 52.13—53.12) is the longest, and, for our purposes, the best source of information about the Servant. It interprets a particular event in the light of existing expectations about the Servant, but the text is enigmatic in many places and must be read in the light of the other three songs. People at first rejected a suffering man as a sinner receiving his punishment; this was the Deuteronomists' explanation of sufferings. Then they changed their minds and realized that he was the Servant, their sin bearer. This

Servant song takes an exactly opposite position to the one implied in Exodus 32.30–33, that one person could not make atonement for others, and so must have been composed before, or apart from, the influence of the Deuteronomists in the late seventh century BCE. 'Theologically', then, this Servant song belongs in the time of the First-Isaiah.

> Surely he has borne, *nāśā'*, our griefs/sicknesses and carried
>   our sorrows/pains;
> Yet we esteemed him stricken, smitten by God and afflicted.
>
> (Isa. 53.4)

There have been many suggestions as to whose suffering prompted the fourth song; the most likely person is king Hezekiah.[67] During his reign, the threatening Assyrian army was destroyed by bubonic plague near Jerusalem. People said the angel of the LORD had killed them (Isa. 37.36), because the plague was a sign of divine wrath. Since Hezekiah had a boil that responded to a fig poultice, an ancient treatment for plague boils (Isa. 38.21), it seems that he also caught the plague and was about to die when Isaiah visited him.

Three accounts survive in the Bible of this incident in the summer of 700 BCE (Isa. 37—38; 2 Kings 19—20; 2 Chron. 32), and the texts are somewhat disordered. Hezekiah prayed for deliverance for his threatened city (Isa. 37.14–20), and Isaiah's first response was the warning that the king would die (Isa. 38.1). Then the prophet received a second revelation and returned to the king (Isa. 38.4; 2 Kings 20.4) to say that he would survive and the city would be saved (Isa. 37.21–35; 38.6). At this point the Assyrian army was destroyed by plague. The present order of the text (the destruction of the Assyrian army in Isaiah 38 and the sickness of Hezekiah in Isaiah 39) implies that Hezekiah became sick *after* the demise of the Assyrians, whereas the original order had him taken ill while they were still threatening the city.

Isaiah had at first assumed that the king's plague was divine wrath, punishment for destroying the LORD's rural shrines. The Assyrian envoys had taunted the people of the city: 'But if you say to me, "We

---

[67] See my article 'Hezekiah's Boil', *Journal for the Study of the Old Testament* 95 (2001), pp. 31–42.

rely on the LORD our God," is it not he whose high places and altars Hezekiah has removed, saying to Judah and to Jerusalem, "You shall worship before this altar in Jerusalem"' (2 Kings 18.22). Then Isaiah realized that the king's plague showed he was the Servant, and so had borne the sin of his city. As he recovered, so the city would be saved. The fourth Servant song was written to celebrate this deliverance, and the king's suffering was interpreted in the light of what Isaiah believed about the Servant. The song is the earliest evidence for the role of the Servant.

> Behold, my servant shall prosper,
> He shall be exalted and lifted up,
> And shall be very high.
>
> (Isa. 52.13)

The LORD spoke (through his prophet?) and so the Servant was introduced as 'my Servant'. In the Lxx he was *pais*, as in Acts and the *Didache*, but in the post-Christian translations by Aquila and Symmachus (hereafter A and S), he was *doulos*, as in the Philippians hymn. In the Isaiah Targum he was 'my Servant the Messiah'. '[He] shall prosper' (RSV) or 'be prudent' (AV) should be translated 'he will have insight/understand', the other meaning for the Hebrew verb *śākal*, and how it was understood by the Greek translators: the Lxx chose 'shall understand', *sunēsei*, and A chose 'shall be made to have knowledge', *epistēmonisthēsetai*. Thus too the writer of the Qumran *Thanksgiving Hymns*:

> O LORD who hast given understanding
> to the heart of [thy] Servant
> that he may understand all these things . . .[68]

The Servant would be wise, and 'exalted and lifted up', the verbs used to describe the LORD himself in Isaiah's vision (Isa. 6.1). We recognize a temple mystic.

> As many were astonished at him –
> His appearance was so marred,
> Beyond human semblance,
> And his form beyond that of the sons of men –
>
> (Isa. 52.14)

---

[68] *Thanksgiving Hymns*, 1QH VI.

This verse has significantly different forms in the ancient versions. The MT and the Targum, which used the MT, say he was disfigured beyond human semblance, such that people were astonished (thus RSV). The Qumran Isaiah scroll,[69] however, has 'he was *anointed* beyond human semblance' such that kings and people were astonished. The difference is one letter: *mšḥt* in the MT and *mšḥty* in the Qumran scroll. The Servant 'anointed beyond human semblance' means he was transfigured, and so, as did Enoch, he became like one of the glorious ones. The Targum mentions this later, that the Servant would look different from an ordinary man because he would have a holy brightness, *ziyw*.[70]

> *So shall he startle many nations;*
> Kings shall shut their mouths because of him;
> For that which has not been told them they shall see
> And that which they have not heard they shall understand.
>
> (Isa. 52.15)

The Servant 'startles' many nations, thus AV and RSV, but the MT actually has 'sprinkles', *yazzeh*, the action of the high priest on the day of atonement (Lev. 16.14 has the same word).[71] The Greek of Aquila also has 'sprinkle', *rhantisei*. Then the kings were astonished and recognized him, as they recognized the Chosen One in *1 Enoch* 48 and 62.

The opening lines of the song reveal a now-familiar figure: anointed and transfigured, raised up and given knowledge. Then, as high priest on the day of atonement, he sprinkles many nations. This perhaps was his ultimate role: to bring atonement and renewal for more than just the people of Jerusalem and Judah. Isaiah then spoke of the Servant who was unexpectedly revealed, in other words, the one whom we have already met as the hidden one in *1 Enoch*.

> Who has believed what we have heard?
> And to whom has the arm of the LORD been revealed?
> For he grew up before him like a young plant,

---

[69] 1QIsaª.

[70] Targum to Isaiah 53.2.

[71] This too Aquila and another post-Christian Greek version by Theodotion, also the Latin Vulgate.

And like a root out of dry ground;
He had no form or comeliness that we should look at him,
And no beauty that we should desire him.
He was despised and rejected by men;
A man of sorrows, and acquainted with grief;
And as one from whom men hide their faces
He was despised, and we esteemed him not.

(Isa. 53.1–3)

'To whom has the arm of the LORD been revealed?' is better read as 'to whom has the seed/son of the LORD been revealed?', since the Hebrew word *zera'* means either, and 'son' fits better with the next line which actually says: 'he grew up before him like a suckling child', rather than 'young plant' as in RSV. The Lxx has 'little child', *paidion*. The root in a dry land would then refer to the royal title used of Jesus 'the root and offspring of David, the bright Morning Star' (Rev. 22.16).[72] Thus too the letters of 53.10, 'he shall see his offspring' can be read as 'he shall be revealed as the son', just as the Chosen One was revealed in the *Parables of Enoch*.[73] The words 'form', *to'ar*, and 'comeliness', *hādār*, may be wordplay, because *to'ar* means, literally, 'a shape drawn in outline', and so similar to *d^{e}mut*; and *hādār* would be better translated 'majesty' or 'splendour'. These the Servant lacked, and yet the Targum emphasized the opposite: 'His appearance shall not be that of a common man, nor the fear of him that of an ordinary man; but his brightness shall be a holy brightness . . .' The Servant was afflicted with sorrows and grief, which the Lxx translated as 'a man with plague', presumably remembering Hezekiah.

Then the people and the prophet changed their minds. The Servant now seems to be contrasted with Ezekiel's *cherub*, the heavenly Adam figure who was driven from Eden. Ezekiel's anointed *cherub* walked in Eden and had been created as the Seal of the plan. S/he was a being of beauty and wisdom, until s/he was filled with violence. The *cherub* was thrown down (literally made unholy/profaned, *hll*) because of violence and iniquity; kings stared, and all the peoples were appalled at the *cherub*'s fate (Ezek. 28.12–19).

---

[72] See above, p. 102.
[73] *1 Enoch* 48.7; 62.7; 69.26.

> Surely he has borne our griefs
> And carried our sorrows;
> Yet we esteemed him stricken, smitten by God, and afflicted.
> *But he was wounded for our transgressions,*
> *He was bruised for our iniquities;*
> *Upon him was the chastisement that made us whole,*
> *And with his stripes we are healed.*
> All we like sheep have gone astray;
> We have turned every one to his own way;
> And the LORD has laid on him
> The iniquity of us all.   (Isa. 53.4–6)

The Servant bore our griefs/pains and carried our sorrows/sickness; in each case the Hebrew word has a range of meanings.[74] The Servant was 'wounded', but this is the verb *ḥll*, used for the profaned *cherub*, and so could mean that the Servant too was 'made unholy/profaned' – but not by his own iniquity. 'He was profaned by *our* transgressions, smitten by *our* iniquities'. Later we read, v. 9, that unlike the *cherub*, the Servant had done no violence, and, as we shall see, he too was the Seal. The song began by saying that kings and peoples were amazed at what they saw. There are too many similarities of theme and language between Ezekiel's dirge for the *cherub* and Isaiah's song of the Servant for this to be coincidence. The Adam who prompted Ezekiel's oracle also lay behind Isaiah's poem.

Isaiah realized that the suffering man was the sin bearer, and the mid-point of the poem shows what this means: 'Upon him was the chastisement that made us whole, and with his stripes we are healed' (Isa. 53.5b). Here Isaiah uses with vivid effect the double meanings that characterized temple tradition. These same words can also mean: 'the covenant bond of our peace was upon him, and by his joining us together we are healed'. This is the wordplay:

- In the first translation 'chastisement' is *mwsr*, pronounced *musār*; in the second translation 'covenant bond' is *mwsr*, the same letters but pronounced *mōsēr*, as in Ezekiel 20.37.
- In the first translation 'stripes' is *ḥbrt*, pronounced *ḥabburōt*, which is the less common meaning of the word; in the second translation, 'joining us together' is *ḥbrt*, the same letters but pronounced *ḥoberet*,

---

[74] Matthew (8.17) saw this fulfilled in Jesus' ministry of healing.

meaning the device for joining the curtains of the tabernacle (Exod. 26.10, 'loops'). This word is formed from the primary meaning of the root *ḥbr*, which is 'to join'.

The responsibility of the Servant was to restore the covenant of peace, and thus to heal by restoring unity. On the day of atonement, this was done by cleansing and consecrating the polluted temple, which was remembered as the context of the Servant song. The Targum here depicts the Servant as the high priest on the day of atonement:

> Then he shall pray on behalf of our transgressions, and our iniquities shall be pardoned for his sake, though we were accounted smitten, stricken from before the LORD and afflicted.
> But he shall build the sanctuary that was polluted because of our transgressions and given up because of our iniquities; and by his teaching shall his peace be multiplied upon us and by our devotion to his words our transgressions shall be forgiven us.[75]

'The covenant bond of our peace' and 'joining together' means that the Servant, like Ezekiel's *cherub*, was the Seal.[76] In the lines after the first song, the Servant's role as the seal was described as his being 'a covenant to the people' (Isa. 42.6). He was also a light to the nations and had to open blind eyes and set prisoners free. The same sequence follows the second song: he was a covenant to the people and had to set prisoners free (Isa. 49.8–9). Opening eyes (with his light) and setting prisoners free (with his restored covenant) also follows the self-proclamation of the Anointed One in Isaiah 61, even though the word 'Servant' does not occur. This was the prophecy Jesus claimed to fulfil (Luke 4.16–21), and it was the key prophecy in the Qumran Melchizedek text, where Melchizedek would set his people free from the evil one, Belial, and make the great atonement. All these are trails that lead back to the Servant/Melchizedek, and link him to Jesus.

The restoration of the covenant and the cleansing were done through the Servant's suffering because the LORD laid on him the iniquity, *'awōn*, of others. The LORD 'laid on him' is a verb that occurs also in Isaiah 53.12, and it means literally 'intercept' or 'interpose', just as Aaron put himself between the sinful people and the wrath (Lev.

---

[75] Targum to Isaiah 53.4–5.

[76] So too Zerubbabel, 'my servant ... I shall make you like a seal, for I have chosen you ...' (Hag. 2.23, my translation).

16.47–48). When the Servant intercepted the iniquity that polluted the temple and broke the covenant, he had the role of the scapegoat, or rather, the scapegoat had the role of the Servant. The Servant in the song carried the iniquity until he offered himself as the *'āshām*, which was the special sacrifice for restoring the covenant (Isa. 53.10).

Here the mystery is impenetrable, although the earliest Christians understood it, or, at the very least, knew about it. The Servant had the roles of *both* goats on the day of atonement: he poured himself out, like the goat whose blood was taken into the holy of holies, and he bore the sins, like the second goat who was driven away. The *Mishnah* emphasized that both goats had to be identical in every way, and maybe this is why; both represented a single figure. In the time of the First-Isaiah, people would have known what modern scholars call 'gemination', the belief that great figures were represented in double form. The crown prince at Ugarit (some time before Isaiah!) had been called the Morning Star and the Evening Star, two aspects or functions of Venus.[77] The king of Assyria, whose armies besieged Jerusalem in the time of the First-Isaiah, was depicted as two identical figures on either side of the tree of life.[78] The composer of the Servant songs would have known about gemination, but not by that name.

The *Letter of Barnabas* is an early Christian text attributed to the Levite Barnabas who was a companion of St Paul (Acts 4.36; 13.1). Presumably he knew about gemination too, because he compared Jesus to both goats. At the end of the second temple period, according to the *Mishnah*, they used to tie red wool to the horns of the scapegoat and pull out its hair as it was driven away.[79] Barnabas gave more detail than the *Mishnah*, and said the animal was goaded and spat upon as it was driven away. He was identifying the scapegoat as the Servant, because in the third song, the Servant speaks of his suffering:

> I gave my back to the smiters,
> and my cheeks to those who pulled out the beard;
> I hid not my face from shame and spitting.   (Isa. 50.6)

---

[77] For them a male deity.

[78] There are examples of these in the Nineveh Gallery of the British Museum, double figures as mirror images, depicting one king.

[79] Mishnah *Yoma* 6.4, 6.

But Barnabas also saw Jesus as the sacrificed goat: 'When they see him coming on the Day, they are going to be struck with terror at the manifest parallel between him and the goat.' The sacrificed goat prefigured for Barnabas the LORD returning on the day of judgement, just as the high priest emerged each year bringing the blood of the goat to renew the creation.[80]

Justin knew this too. In his *Dialogue with Trypho*, a Jew, he wrote:

> The two goats which were ordered to be offered during the fast, of which one was sent away as the scapegoat and the other sacrificed were similarly declarative of the two appearances of Christ: the first in which the elders of your people, and the priests, having laid hands on him and put him to death, sent him away as the scapegoat; and his second appearance, because in the same place in Jerusalem you shall recognize him who you have dishonoured and who was an offering for all sinners willing to repent . . .[81]

This was not forgotten. Cyril of Alexandria wrote in the early fifth century: 'We must perceive the Immanuel in the slaughtered goat . . . the two goats illustrate the mystery,'[82] and this was the mystery of the Servant.

> He was oppressed, and he was afflicted,
> Yet he opened not his mouth;
> Like a lamb that is led to the slaughter,
> And like a sheep that before its shearers is dumb,
> So he opened not his mouth.
> By oppression and judgement he was taken away;
> And as for his generation, who considered
> That he was cut off out of the land of the living,
> Stricken for the transgression of my people?
> *And they made his grave with the wicked*
> *And with a rich man in his death,*
> Although he had done no violence,
> And there was no deceit in his mouth.
> (Isa. 53.7–9, my emphasis)

Although the detail of the original Hebrew is lost, motifs from the day of atonement have been preserved here by the Targum. The suffering

---

[80] *Letter of Barnabas* 7.
[81] Justin, *Dialogue with Trypho* 40.
[82] Cyril of Alexandria, *Letter* 41.

of the Servant was extended to include the suffering of the people in exile, as when the Second-Isaiah reworked the Servant songs into their new context. The Servant brought the exiles home. This is found in the lines after the second song: 'to raise up the tribes of Jacob and to restore the preserved of Israel . . .' (Isa. 49.6).[83] The return of the scattered people was part of the Jubilee that was proclaimed on the day of atonement (Lev. 25.8–10).

> Out of chastisement and out of punishment shall he bring our exiles near, and the wondrous things that shall be wrought for us in his days, who shall be able to recount? For he shall take away the dominion of the peoples from the land of Israel, and the sins which my people sinned shall he transfer to them.[84]

'His grave with the wicked', and his death with the rich man are opaque in their present form, although the 'rich man' was recognized as a prophecy of Joseph of Arimathea who gave his tomb for Jesus (Mark 15.42–47). The Hebrew words 'wicked', *ršʿ*, pronounced *rāshāʿ*, and 'rich', *ʿšyr*, pronounced *ʿāshiyr*, are both written with the same letters, and these are also the letters for goat, *śʿyr*, pronounced *sāʿiyr*.[85] Since reordering letters was one of the methods of the correcting scribes, and since the context of this Servant song is the day of atonement, one wonders if the words were originally 'goats' and 'goat' respectively. The letters of 'grave', *qbr*, with a similar reordering, become *qrb*, a temple offering.[86] The original may have been 'He gave the goats for his offering and the goat for his death.'[87]

> Yet it was the will of the LORD to bruise him;
> He has put him to grief;
> When he makes himself an offering for sin,
> He shall see his offspring, he shall prolong his days;
> *The will of the LORD shall prosper in his hand;*
> *He shall see the fruit of the travail of his soul and be satisfied;*
> *By his knowledge shall the Righteous One, my Servant,*
> *Make many to be accounted righteous;*
> And he shall bear their iniquities.

---

[83] Lxx here has 'cause the diaspora to come back . . .'

[84] Targum to Isaiah 53.8.

[85] The letters š and ś would look the same in an unpointed text.

[86] The Hebrew equivalent of the Aramaic word used for the self offering of the Man in Daniel's vision (Dan. 7.13).

[87] Translating *bᵉ*, as in Exodus 6.3, 'I appeared *as* El Shaddai . . .'

Therefore I will divide him a portion with the great,
And he shall divide the spoil with the strong;
Because he poured out his soul to death,
And was numbered with the transgressors;
Yet he bore the sin of many,
And made intercession for the transgressors.

(Isa. 53.10–12, my emphasis)

There are problems too in this last section. 'It was the will of the LORD to bruise him' became in the LXX 'the LORD wished to purify him from his plague', because the Hebrew word 'bruise', *dk'*, looks the same as the Aramaic word 'purify', and the translators read the text that way. The MT is not clear: v. 10. is literally 'The LORD was pleased to crush him with sickness when you made his soul an offering for sin' and then possibly, 'he shall be revealed as the son and have length of days', as with Enoch's Man.[88]

At this point, there is an additional word in the Qumran scroll – 'light' – which changes the line to: 'After the sorrow/trouble of his soul he will see the light and be satisfied/filled with his knowledge.' The LXX has 'to show him light and to form him with knowledge/understanding . . .', showing that 'light' was in the pre-Christian Hebrew text. With different division of the lines, the text is:

The will/pleasure of the LORD shall prosper in his hand,
After the sorrow/trouble of his soul he will see light and
be satisfied/filled [? with light],
And by his knowledge shall the Righteous One, my
Servant, make many righteous,
And he shall bear their iniquities.

The additional word 'light', *'wr*, and the additional letter in 52.14 change this Servant song into the prophecy on the road to Emmaus. 'Was it not necessary that the Anointed One should suffer these things and enter into his glory?' It is likely that these four letters were not additions to the song, but were removed to sever the link between Isaiah's Servant and Jesus.[89] The Qumran text of Isaiah shows the

---

[88] *1 Enoch* 71.17.

[89] The Psalmist sang of his sufferings, and then claimed: 'As for me, I shall behold [in a vision] thy face in righteousness, and when I wake I shall be satisfied [the same verb *śb'*] with thy form' (Ps. 17.15, my translation). The LXX here has 'I shall be satisfied by seeing your glory'.

Servant as a temple mystic who sees the light and is given knowledge. John described him as the Servant/Lamb who had been killed and raised to life, who had received the sevenfold light and the sevenfold Spirit, and then received the sealed scroll when he was enthroned.

The Servant, the Righteous One, was then able to make others righteous. He did this in two ways; he took away the effect of their sins, and he gave right teaching. This restored the covenant bonds and brought people back within them. The duty of the high priests had been to uphold and restore the covenant, and also, as Malachi reminded his contemporaries, to give right teaching (Mal. 2.4–9). The knowledge given to the temple mystic as he stood before the throne was knowledge about the whole creation, and so the Servant was able to keep people within the bonds of the eternal/creation covenant. Peter described Jesus as the Servant, the Righteous One and the Author of Life, when his theme was the day of atonement (Acts 3.13–15). The Servant in the song poured out his soul to death, a reference to the blood pouring at the end of the atonement ritual, and he was reckoned with the transgressors. He bore the sin of many and, bearing in mind the nuances of the verb used in 53.6, the sense of the last line is 'he intercepted their transgressions'.

To complete Isaiah's picture of the Servant, we consider the other songs. We have seen from the second that he was the hidden one (Isa. 49.2) and from the third that he was tormented (Isa. 50.6). The first song (Isa. 42.1–4 or possibly 1–7) adds two details to the picture and links the Servant back to the royal figure in the oracles of the First-Isaiah, and forward to the baptism of Jesus, who heard the words of this song at his baptism (Mark 1.11 and parallels).

> Behold my Servant, whom I uphold,
> My chosen, in whom my soul delights;
> I have put my Spirit upon him,
> *He will bring forth justice to the nations.*
> He will not cry or lift up his voice,
> Or make it heard in the street;
> A bruised reed he will not break,
> And a dimly burning wick he will not quench;
> *He will faithfully bring forth justice.*
> He will not fail or be discouraged
> *Till he has established justice in the earth.*
>
> (Isa. 42.1–4, my emphasis)

First, the Servant received the Spirit and his role was to bring forth justice, *mishpat*. He was the lawgiver, and so, presumably, the king. 'Bringing forth' justice described the Servant emerging from the holy of holies after the blood offering and enthronement, when he was the LORD coming to judge sinners and atone the land (Deut. 32.43). The one anointed with the manifold Spirit of the LORD had a different type of knowledge because he had received the Spirit of wisdom and understanding, counsel and might, knowledge and the fear of the LORD (Isa. 11.2). Isaiah paired the two words 'justice and righteousness' to describe the peace, *shalōm*, of the restored covenant (Isa. 32, esp. vv. 15–17), and so the Anointed One judged with righteousness. In other words, he was the Righteous One, and he restored harmony to the creation: 'the wolf shall dwell with the lamb . . . for the earth shall be full of the knowledge of the LORD . . .' (Isa. 11.6, 9). The king who was the Righteous One was Melchi-Zedek, 'king of righteousness'.

Second, the Servant was compared to a branched lamp that had been broken. One of the symbols of the Davidic kings was a lamp. Rehoboam, David's grandson, lost the allegiance of all the tribes but was allowed to keep one, 'that David my servant may always have a lamp, *niyr*, before me in Jerusalem . . .' (1 Kings 11.36); and the LORD protected Judah 'for the sake of David his servant, since he promised to give a lamp, *niyr*, to him and to his sons for ever' (2 Kings 8.19; also 2 Sam. 21.17). The branches of the menorah were described as *qāniym*, a word whose primary meaning was 'hollow reed' (Exod. 25.32), and the Servant was described with the same word: he was a 'bruised reed'. Since the next line has a 'wick', the imagery here is the Servant as a branch of the lamp (Isa. 42.3). Repointing the verbs in this line, without changing the letters, gives a perfect parallel to the next verse, and reveals the Servant not as the one who protects a lamp ('a bruised reed he will not break'), but as the one who *is* the lamp.

- *yšbwr*, pronounced *yishbōr*, meaning 'break' becomes the niph'al form pronounced *yishshābēr*, and meaning 'be broken' or 'allow himself to be broken'.
- *ykbnh*, pronounced *yekabbennāh*,[90] meaning 'extinguish', becomes the qal form pronounced *yikbeh*, meaning 'be extinguished'.

---

[90] The 'n' is not part of the verb, just an additional emphasis.

Verse 42.3 is then read:

> A bruised lamp-branch, he will not be broken, a spluttering wick, he will not be extinguished, he will faithfully bring forth justice.

Verse 42.4, translating literally, is:

> He will not burn dimly or be crushed, until he establishes justice on earth, and the coastlands wait for his law.

The two verses are parallel, a Hebrew literary style.

The menorah was a complex temple symbol that represented Wisdom and the tree of life. If the Servant was one branch of the menorah, he was a child of Wisdom. John saw Jesus as the central stem of the menorah, 'one like a son of man in the middle of the lamps' (Rev. 1.13, my translation), and Jesus himself said 'I am the light of the world' (John 8.12). There was, however, a curious silence about the menorah in later texts: the sages who loved to find significance in every small detail of the holy books, especially the Law, said little about the lamp. Scholars have suspected that the lamp was the subject of mystical speculation, which would explain the silence in 'public' texts.

The First-Isaiah pronounced a series of oracles about the royal house, of which his call vision can be considered the first. He saw the LORD as the king (Isa. 6.5), and realized that there had been wrong teaching: 'I am a man of unclean lips, and I dwell in the midst of a people of unclean lips.' As a mystic standing by the throne, he learned that the land was desolate because the people had lost their perception; they had failed to see, to hear and to understand. They had lost Wisdom, and this state would continue until the broken tree with the holy seed was restored to the land.

The second announced the imminent birth of this holy seed: the Virgin, the mother of the LORD,[91] would bear a son and call him Immanuel, 'God with us' (Isa. 7.10–14).

The third announced the birth of the royal child in the glory of the holy ones and gave his four throne names (Isa. 9.6–7).

---

[91] This is the Qumran form of Isaiah 7.11, 'Ask a sign from the Mother of the LORD your God', 1QIsaᵃ.

The fourth announced the gift of the Spirit to the anointed one so that his mind would be transformed and he would be able to restore peace to the earth – 'the knowledge of the LORD' (Isa. 11.1–9).

The temple context of the royal oracles was the ritual birth of the Davidic king described in Psalm 110. The historical context was the threat from the invading Assyrians, and Isaiah interpreted current events in the light of temple expectations. The same was true of the Servant songs, which were also royal oracles. Their temple context was the day of atonement when the royal high priest, who 'was' the LORD with his people, symbolically offered himself to renew the creation. The detail of the Jerusalem festival is lost apart from the songs, but the ancient Mesopotamian Akitu festival was still observed in Isaiah's time, when the cosmos was renewed at new year. The king was ritually humbled before the god and then his regalia was restored to him. Something similar in Jerusalem would explain the Servant songs. The first three songs could have been part of the temple rite but the fourth has been adapted to specific circumstances, as we have seen. All four were re-used by the Second-Isaiah in yet another context.

Not all the elements of the fourth song fit the application to Hezekiah. He is unlikely, for example, to have taken spoil from an army that was destroyed by plague. The fate of the Assyrian army and the spoil is probably described in Isaiah 10.15–17, the LORD sending a wasting sickness among (the king of Assyria's) warriors and kindling fire under his glory. Sharing spoils must have been the role of the original Servant. Now the king had four throne names: Wonderful Counsellor, Mighty God, Everlasting Father (or Father of Booty), Prince of Peace, and these corresponded, as we have seen, to the later names of the four archangels.[92] Further, these four archangels were themselves ways of describing the presence of the LORD. All four can be found in the fourth Servant song, describing who he was and what he did, and accounting for various elements in the song.

- He would have understanding and knowledge (Isa. 52.13; 53.11); the Wonderful Counsellor.

---

[92] See above, p. 67.

- He would be exalted and anointed, and he would cause kings to marvel (Isa. 52.13–15); the Mighty God.
- He would divide the spoils (Isa. 53.12); the Father of Booty.
- He would restore the covenant of peace and make many righteous (Isa. 53.5, 11); the Prince of Peace.

The Christians considered both the royal oracles and the Servant songs together; they were all about one figure and they were all prophecies of Jesus. In Matthew's Gospel, which originated in a Hebrew Christian community, seven of the eight are used, and in the rest of the New Testament, there are many quotations and allusions.

- Isaiah 6.9–10 is cited at Matthew 13.14–15.
- Isaiah 7.14 is cited at Matthew 1.12.
- Isaiah 9.1–2 is cited at Matthew 4.15–16.
- Isaiah 11.1 is (probably) cited at Matthew 2.23.
- Isaiah 42.1 is cited at Matthew 3.17 and 17.6.
- Isaiah 42.1–4 is cited in Matthew 12.18–21.
- [Isaiah 49.6 is cited at Luke 2.32.]
- Isaiah 50.6 is alluded to in Matthew 26.67–68.
- Isaiah 53.3 is cited at Matthew 8.17.
- Isaiah 53.7 is alluded to in Matthew 27.12–14.
- Isaiah 53.9 is alluded to in Matthew 27.59–60.
- Isaiah 53.12 is alluded to in Matthew 26.28.

John presented Jesus as the Servant in a different way, not using quotations from, or allusions to, the Servant texts. He set the Servant in his temple context as the Lamb who takes away the sin of the world (John 1.29); the Son of God who has received the Spirit (John 1.33–34); the Messiah (John 1.41); the King of Israel (John 1.49); the son of man (John 1.51). Jesus was Melchizedek, because he offered wine instead of water at Cana, and thus showed his glory (John 2.1–11). (Philo said Melchizedek offered wine instead of water.[93]) The most telling example of John's style was his account of Jesus and Pilate, which is full of irony, of proofs that the Jews had lost touch with their ancient faith, and of images of the Servant.

---

[93] Philo, *Allegorical Interpretation*, III.82.

Jesus came out, wearing the crown of thorns and the purple robe. Pilate said to [the Jews], 'Behold the man!'

The Jews answered him, 'We have a law, and by that law he ought to die, because he has made himself the Son of God' . . .

[Pilate] said to the Jews, 'Behold your king!'

The chief priests answered, 'We have no king but Caesar.'

(John 19.5, 7, 14, 15)

Postscript

Temple mysticism has been obscured at so many crucial phases in the history of Hebrew and Christian belief.

First, there were the purges instigated by the Deuteronomists and their heirs, a movement akin to the Reformation that changed the face of Europe. The older faith did not die; it survived elsewhere and gradually returned to its ancient places. Since it was the heirs to the 'reformers' who dominated the collection, transmission and final choice of the texts that became the canon of Hebrew scripture, the other voices were only heard as echoes.

Second, as the Church defined itself, there was the need to distinguish between Christianity and Gnosis, even though teachers, who were later labelled 'gnostic', had played a major part in Christian communities. Some thought that Valentinus, teaching in Rome in the mid-second century, would be made bishop there. Early gnostic thought had much in common with temple mysticism, suggesting that pre-Christian Gnosticism had its roots in the older faith.

Third, there was pressure in the Church for Christians not to practise Jewish customs or to revert to them. As the communities grew apart, so the temple roots of Christianity were less well understood, and Judaism itself was changed after the destruction of the temple and the wars against Rome. In the earliest years of Christianity, the Jews were the main persecutors of the Christians and burned their books, and so nothing of 'Hebrew Christianity' survives in Hebrew, or if it does (perhaps among the Dead Sea Scrolls), it has not been identified as such.

Then there were the unacknowledged assumptions of more recent scholarship. Despite the ancient evidence that temple teaching influenced Pythagoras and Plato, which was accepted for centuries at face value, more recent fashion in scholarship has dismissed the idea. In 1517 J. Reuchlin wrote: 'Pythagoras brought this teaching to Greece, along with the rest of the Kabbalah ... If I declare that Kabbalah and Pythagoreanism are of the same stuff, I will not be departing from facts.'[1]

---

[1] J. Reuchlin, *On the Art of Kabbalah*, Book 2, 1517, tr. M. and S. Goodman, Lincoln, NE: University of Nebraska Press, 1993.

170

Many New Testament scholars, however, had been trained as classicists rather than Hebraists, and so they identified familiar elements in early Christianity as Platonism rather than temple tradition.

It was fashionable for a long time for Protestant or Free Church scholars, who dominated the field for many years, to dismiss as ridiculous anything that did not conform to their modern view of what the original Christianity *must* have been. 'Gnostic' and non-canonical material thus had less value than canonical texts for reconstructing Christian origins, even though it was increasingly clear that the Hebrew text underlying English translations of the Old Testament could not have been the text that Jesus and the first Christians knew.

Their conclusions were often implied in their premises and in what evidence they would admit. Thus R. P. C. Hanson, in books published some 50 years ago, could write of Clement of Alexandria:

> Clement's teaching did, as far as we can reconstruct it, consist of speculations, intuitions and inspired (or not so inspired) theologizing, which had no connection with any oral teaching given by our Lord and his apostles.[2]

Of Basil the Great's teaching about the unwritten traditions in the Church he wrote:

> At first sight this looks like an attempt to turn Christianity into a mystery-religion or an ecclesiastical freemasonry and to canonize a tradition of custom which earlier Christian ages had regarded as wholly secondary . . .
>
> Behind this unfortunate and wholly unjustifiable claim for a genuine apostolic origin for the liturgical and customary practice of the contemporary Church lies *an uncertainty about how to use biblical material.*[3]

How did he know?

In a similar vein were the conclusions in a contemporary publication: M. D. Hooker's study *Jesus and the Servant.* She concluded that the central figure in temple mysticism was not significant in the foundation of Christian theology, when in fact, as we have seen, the Servant was fundamental. She concluded:

---

[2] R. P. C. Hanson, *Origen's Doctrine of Tradition*, London: SPCK, 1954, p. 71.

[3] R. P. C. Hanson, *Tradition in the Early Church*, London: SCM Press, 1962, p. 184, my emphases.

There is, therefore, very little in the Synoptics to support the trad-itional view that Jesus identified his mission with that of the Servant of the Songs: certainly there is nothing that could be accepted as proof for this view.

Our study has revealed that there is little evidence that Servant-Christology held any important place in Christian thought of the New Testament period . . . Further study has not revealed that the idea held any great significance for the early Church.[4]

This further study has concluded exactly the opposite!

'Go and say to this people: "Hear and hear, but do not understand; see and see, but do not perceive."'   (Isa. 6.9)

---

[4] M. D. Hooker, *Jesus and the Servant*, London: SPCK, 1959, pp. 102, 128.

Index of biblical and ancient texts

ND - #0047 - 270325 - C0 - 216/138/13 - PB - 9780281064830 - Gloss Lamination